HIV and Aids in Schools

HIV and Aids in Schools

The Political Economy of Pressure Groups
and Miseducation

BARRIE CRAVEN
PAULINE DIXON
GORDON STEWART
JAMES TOOLEY

The Institute of Economic Affairs

First published in Great Britain in 2001 by
The Institute of Economic Affairs
2 Lord North Street
Westminster
London SW1P 3LB
in association with Profile Books Ltd

A CIP catalogue record for this book is available from the British Library.

ISBN 0 255 36522 5

Many IEA publications are translated into languages other than English or are
reprinted. Permission to translate or to reprint should be sought from the
General Director at the address above.

Typeset in Stone by MacGuru
info@macguru.org.uk

Printed and bound in Great Britain by Hobbs the Printers

CONTENTS

THE AUTHORS

Barrie M. Craven

Dr Craven is Reader in Public Accountability at Newcastle Business School (University of Northumbria). He is a graduate of the University of Hull and the University of Newcastle upon Tyne. He has published in the field of monetary economics in the *Journal of Monetary Economics*, the *Manchester School* and the *European Journal of Finance*. More recently he has researched public policy and healthcare issues. Current research is focused on the resource strategies associated with healthcare issues, where results are published in several journals, including the *Journal of Public Policy* and *Financial Accountability and Management*. Other recent publications are in the area of food safety and regulation. He has taught at Curtin University, Western Australia, and at Cal. Poly in California. He visited Moscow and Uralsk in the early 1990s to teach business people about the working of capitalism. His main teaching interest is in the field of international trade documentation and finance.

Pauline Dixon

Pauline Dixon graduated from the Open University with a first-class honours degree and diplomas in music and economics. She is currently undertaking a doctorate at the University of Newcastle upon Tyne in education policy under the supervision of Professor James Tooley. Her main interests are the regulatory environment and the economic philosophies of the Austrian School. She also lectures in economics at the University of Northumbria. Although she considers herself a microeconomist, she has also lectured in macroeconomics and industrial economics. Pauline's research examines the regulatory environment of private schools in developing countries, considering the current position from an Austrian economic stance. Her aim is to influence regulatory policy in developing countries in order to nurture and stimulate private schools for the poor.

Gordon Stewart

Gordon Stewart retired as Professor of Public Health and Head of the Department of Epidemiology at Glasgow University in 1984.

Stewart qualified in medicine at Glasgow in 1942. He saw service in the Arctic and tropics in the Royal Navy during World War II, and then worked in hospitals and medical schools in the UK until 1963, when he was offered a post in the USA as Professor of Epidemiology at the University of North Carolina, Chapel Hill, NC. In 1968, he became head of the corresponding department at Tulane University Medical Center in New Orleans. In 1972, he returned to Glasgow.

Until 1963, his main professional interest was in the epidemiology and control of communicable diseases and development of antimicrobial drugs and vaccines. Since then, his interest has extended beyond the usual infectious diseases to disorders like the abuse of alcohol, smoking, addictive drugs and health-damaging lifestyles, which are communicable by peer pressures and patterns of behaviour. Since retirement, he has worked for the WHO and various other health and educational authorities as a consultant, mainly in these subjects, with a special focus on Aids, in the UK, North America, the Middle East and Africa.

James Tooley

James Tooley is Professor of Education Policy at the University of Newcastle, England. Prior to this he was Senior Research Fellow in the School of Education, University of Manchester. He is also Director of the Education Programme at the Institute of Economic Affairs, London. Professor Tooley gained his PhD from the Institute of Education, University of London and has held research positions at the University of Oxford's Department of Educational Studies and the National Foundation for Educational Research. He has taught at Simon Fraser University (Canada), the University of the Western Cape (South Africa) and as a mathematics teacher at schools in Zimbabwe. He is a columnist for *Economic Affairs*, and is the author of *Disestablishing the School* (1995), *Education without the State* (1996), *The Higher Education Debate* (1997), *Educational Research: A Critique* (with Doug Darby, 1998), *The Global Education Industry* (1999) and *Reclaiming Education* (2000).

FOREWORD

All schools in this country must include in their curriculum teaching about HIV and Aids, subject to inspection by the Office for Standards in Education (Ofsted). But, as the authors of Occasional Paper 121 point out, schools have discretion in *what* they teach. Barrie Craven, Pauline Dixon, Gordon Stewart and James Tooley show how, in a series of Acts since the Education Reform Act of 1988 which introduced the National Curriculum, while HIV/Aids teaching has become compulsory, schools have been left in the dark about the content of lessons on the subject. The issues are difficult and controversial, even for experts in the field, so it seems most unlikely that secondary school teachers can tackle the subject satisfactorily.

Craven, Dixon, Stewart and Tooley begin with the history of legislation in this field (Chapter 1) and then (Chapter 2) examine the material used by schools in teaching about HIV and Aids, setting out the results of a number of school visits in which they interviewed teachers and attended lessons on the subject. They conclude that the messages reaching children are seriously misleading. Special interest groups appear to be foisting material on teachers who are poorly equipped to judge it. The resulting lessons give the impression that HIV/Aids has reached epidemic proportions and that all are equally at risk, regardless of behaviour.

Craven et al. argue, however, that the scientific evidence shows

no evidence of such an epidemic (Chapter 3). The total number of
HIV cases diagnosed to date in the United Kingdom is 43,000, of
which less than 1 per cent appear to have contracted their infections from heterosexual intercourse where there is no evidence of
a high-risk partner or infection outside Europe. Deaths from Aids
in the UK are very small compared with the major killer diseases –
263 in 2000, compared with 250,000 from cancer and heart disease and 60,000 from pneumonia. Even 'falling down stairs' had
more victims (549).

The Aids situation in Africa, which is often thought to be so
serious as to justify drastic action to avoid a similar 'epidemic' elsewhere, is less clear-cut than generally supposed. According to
Craven et al. (Chapter 4), there are a number of anomalies in the
data which lead them to question the conventional wisdom about
Aids in Africa. In particular, diagnostic standards are different
from those in Britain, and it is possible that many Aids cases are a
reclassification of existing diseases.

From an economic policy viewpoint, Occasional Paper 121
provides evidence to support the arguments of those economists
who claim that rent-seeking by pressure groups is rife and that, in
politicised markets (such as education in this country),
government policies will be unduly influenced by such groups.
Where government intervenes heavily in any market, it invariably
opens up opportunities for groups to lobby for the interests of
their members in the hope of gaining benefits for them at the
expense of the rest of the community. The gains, concentrated on
members, can be huge, and so lobbying is a very high-return
activity on which resources become concentrated. Given the
evidence presented by Craven et al. about the true scale of the
HIV/Aids 'problem', it is hard to see how it could have achieved

11

such prominence in the nation's schools without powerful interest-group pressures. Similarly, the form which teaching takes has, according to Craven et al. (Chapter 5), been strongly influenced by vested interests.

The solution to the present unfortunate state of HIV/Aids education, according to the authors (Chapter 6), is not to prescribe the content of teaching on the subject (which would be difficult, given the controversial nature of the issues). Instead, HIV and Aids should no longer be compulsory subjects in schools. Either the law should be repealed, or parents and school governors should simply drop the subjects in a 'minor act of civil disobedience'.

As in all IEA papers, the views expressed in Occasional Paper 121 are those of the authors, not of the Institute (which has no corporate view), its managing trustees, Academic Advisory Council members or senior staff. The paper is published to encourage debate on the controversial issues with which it deals.

COLIN ROBINSON

Editorial Director, Institute of Economic Affairs
Professor of Economics, University of Surrey

SUMMARY

- When Aids was first recognised in the 1980s it was presented as a serious health threat for which there was no cure. There were fears that it could spread to the heterosexual population. Government felt it must 'do something'.
- The government therefore introduced into all schools in England and Wales a compulsory requirement that they teach about HIV and Aids. But the content of their teaching is not prescribed.
- The issues are difficult and controversial: teachers are ill-equipped to deal with them. Research into what children are taught suggests that the messages they are receiving are seriously misleading.
- The impression is given that there is an HIV/Aids epidemic and that all are equally at risk, regardless of their sexual behaviour.
- However, there is no evidence of such an epidemic. So far about 43,000 HIV cases have been diagnosed in the United Kingdom, very few of which appear to involve infections contracted from heterosexual intercourse except where there is evidence of a high-risk partner or infection outside Europe. There are very few Aids deaths – 263 in 2000.
- It is widely believed that there is an Aids epidemic in Africa but the evidence is not clear-cut. There are numerous

anomalies in the data. Diagnostic standards are different from those in Britain, and many Aids cases may be reclassifications of existing diseases.

- Given the evidence, it is hard to see why HIV and Aids education has such a privileged place in the school curriculum.
- The reason is probably that there are many powerful pressure groups which benefit from the present situation – for example, pharmaceutical companies, health professionals and researchers.
- The solution is *not* to make the content of lessons about HIV and Aids compulsory.
- The law that makes HIV and Aids education compulsory should be repealed, or school governors and parents should simply make sure that their schools drop this part of the curriculum.

TABLES AND FIGURES

INTRODUCTION

Something odd, and rather disturbing, is happening in our schools. All schools are compelled to teach about HIV and Aids. Not doing so is an offence, under the 1996 Education Act. Ofsted even inspects for it; governing bodies are required to make policies about it. However, *what* schools teach about HIV and Aids is *not* similarly prescribed. It is the responsibility of the school itself to gather the information that it is to deliver in its programme. Although vague guidelines are published, no content is provided in any of the government's literature.

What this means in practice is that schools become the target for a whole range of special interest groups, seeing rich pickings if they can get their material into the hands of children. The argument of this paper is that the current situation is a recipe for propaganda and misinformation. Through government action, schools are becoming battlegrounds in a phoney war in which children, along with truth and education, are the casualties.

The paper opens with a description of the development of the law on HIV and Aids education in the context of broader developments in sex education legislation (Chapter 1). It also reviews some of the literature available to schools and teachers to facilitate meeting their statutory obligations.

This is followed in Chapter 2 by short vignettes of the ways in which HIV and Aids are being taught in secondary schools.

Conversations with and between teachers and advisers for the local education authorities (LEAs) are also recounted, together with quotations from published materials and literature with which children were being supplied. Some of this material may be found offensive by readers – but we felt it necessary to include some of it to show the explicitness with which these issues are being discussed with children, government guidelines notwithstanding.

Even if people did not object to the content of what children were receiving, some might wonder whether teachers and LEA advisers know enough about such complex scientific and medical issues to be able to make informed decisions about what material to present to children. How can medically and scientifically unqualified people decide what to present? How can they avoid propaganda? Chapter 3 takes these issues farther, outlining how controversial many of the issues concerning HIV and Aids are. Demographic and statistical evidence, theories and medical information are all analysed and provided to equip the reader with at least some sense of the controversy of the issues, and the one-sidedness and alarmist nature of what is finding its way into schools. But doesn't the situation in sub-Saharan Africa show that we must avoid any complacency? Chapter 4 explores the evidence concerning Aids in Africa and suggests that widely held views on the position there may not be as compelling as is often thought.

Chapter 5 then offers some ideas on why these controversial issues have achieved such priority in the political agenda, before the final chapter draws the issues together, and offers an alternative way forward. One solution which may occur to some readers, of course, would be not only to compel schools to teach about HIV and Aids, but to make the *content* compulsory too. This paper shies away from that possibility. The issues are too controversial.

And controversial issues make for bad state compulsion. The better way, given all that is argued in this paper, is to persuade government to withdraw from this area altogether.

While going through the arguments, the reader might like to reflect on some of the following statistics – undisputed facts concerning HIV, Aids and other health matters – to help bring together his or her own conclusions about what is being taught and why, and to reflect on the current priorities within schools:

- From 1982 until December 2000, 43,834 people (mainly symptom-free) were diagnosed as 'seropositive' (for an explanation see Chapter 3) to HIV in the UK. In low-risk, heterosexually acquired HIV, exposure is presumed to have occurred abroad, mainly in Africa (69 per cent) or with a partner from countries in which Aids is prevalent. Only 10 per cent reported exposure within Europe.[1] Otherwise, in 58 per cent, seropositivity was associated with (male) homosexual intercourse and, in 8 per cent, with injection of addictive drugs.
- In the year 2000, the number of persons diagnosed in clinics in the UK as seropositive to HIV was 2,868. Of these, 630 were females reporting exposure outside Europe, mainly in Africa (68 per cent), or with partners from non-European countries.[2]

1 'Communicable Disease Report', PHLS, vol. 9, no. 22, 28 May 1999, p. 199.
2 In the UK, there is no obligation to record the HIV/Aids status of travellers, visitors and immigrants, or to notify any information whatever to health authorities or to investigate partners or contacts. In many other countries, including the USA and Russia, this information is required by law and admission is discretionary. In the UK, tuberculosis, leprosy and other notifiable diseases must be registered if known but need not be notified onward or acted on by health or local authorities. The result is that many persons with these diseases and all persons with HIV/Aids are unrecognised unless they report sick to a GP or hospital.

- Also in the year 2000, 263 people died from an Aids-defining[3] illness in the UK. This was a continuation of the fall from the peak of 1,533 deaths attributable to Aids in 1994. Although Aids is commonly regarded as a leading hazard to health, it should be noted that, in the year 2000 as in preceding years, about 300,000 people died from cancer and heart disease, that 2,765 women died from lung cancer, 12,677 from breast cancer,[4] and that prostatic cancer kills about 60 times as many men as Aids.

These findings, which are verifiable in the cumulative HIV/Aids Surveillance database maintained by the Public Health Laboratory Service (PHLS), show that Aids in the UK has never been an epidemic and has been since the early 1990s a rare and di-minishing disease except for a continuing incidence in the original risk groups of homo- and bisexual men and users of addictive

---

3 Persons dying with Aids may be classified as HIV Disease under ICD (International Classification of Diseases) 042, or as Aids under 043, or as the Aids-defining diagnosis (e.g. Pneumocystis pneumonia, toxoplasma encephalitis) with HIV Disease as the underlying cause under ICD 044. This can also be used in persons dying from any other cause listed in the ICD. It is admitted by the Office of National Statistics (ONS) that classification of deaths of persons with Aids is ambiguous. In practice, there is no reference to HIV or Aids in the death certificates of many persons dying with HIV disease or Aids because of objections by relatives, contacts and others, or for reasons of political correctness. This leads to under-reporting, which is supposed to be corrected by the Public Health Laboratory Service in Aids/HIV quarterly surveillance tables and in periodic reviews. HIV disease may legitimately be entered as an underlying cause in deaths for any reason of persons who are seropositive. This leads to over-reporting of HIV disease, and is the basis of many claims that deaths from Aids are increasing. In all other deaths, the ONS may seek additional detail but not necessarily or not at all with HIV/Aids. This is left to the PHLS, but there is no record linkage.

4 Nigel Hawkes, 'Big lung cancer rise among women', *The Times*, 25 September 2000.

drugs, usually by injection. But the data also reveal an increase in females, no longer only in the small numbers originally exposed by contacts with bisexual men but much more so in women receiving exposure in countries outside Europe where Aids is very prevalent, or with partners from such countries. This increment is concentrated in London and associated also with a much greater increase in gonorrhoea, chlamydia and several other sexually transmissible infections. Apart from this minor increment, it is predictable from the data presented here and in trends apparent in the PHLS database that Aids would be unlikely to affect the general population of the UK.

1   POLICY AND PRACTICE

A history lesson

Before 1986 schools and LEAs were not under any obligation to provide sex education or placed under any scrutiny with regard to its content. Indeed, the Education (No. 2) Act 1986 gave school governing bodies the autonomy to decide whether or not sex education should be part of the secular curriculum. And sex education, where presented, was required to promote moral values. The school governing bodies were also required to 'make and keep up to date' a written statement of their school's sex education policy (Education (No. 2) Act 1986 s. 18). These provisions were in part to reduce the power of LEAs in sex education, for there had been some media coverage of particular material being promoted in schools which some had deemed inappropriate.

Things began to move on in 1987, as the government and public became increasingly aware of the relatively new disease of Aids and HIV. The DES Circular 11/87, 'Sex Education in schools', expressed the Secretary of State's belief[1] 'that education about Aids is an important element in the teaching programme offered to pupils in the later years of compulsory schooling'.

In 1987, the booklet 'Aids: Some Questions and Answers' was

---

1   As stated in *The Head's Legal Guide*, Croner, 1993, 3–61.

published by the DES, the Welsh, Scottish and Northern Ireland Offices. In its foreword the Secretary of State pointed to the crucial part schools and colleges would play 'in ensuring that young people know the facts about the disease, its risks, and how they can be avoided'.

The Education Reform Act 1988 introduced the National Curriculum. This stated that schools had to provide a curriculum that was balanced and broad (1988 Act (s. 1(2))). It needed to promote 'the spiritual, moral, cultural, mental and physical development of pupils at the school' and prepare pupils for 'the opportunities, responsibilities and experiences of adult life' (s. 1(2)(b)). Although the Act did not make the provision of sex education compulsory, if the above criteria were to be fulfilled some claimed that it made the provision of sex education necessary (Harris, 1996a: 8).

In 1991 the National Curriculum for Science was amended at Key Stage 3 (for children aged eleven to fourteen) to include the study of the 'ways in which the human body can be affected by ... HIV and Aids'. This caused great concern and controversy. It was felt by some, especially among Conservative backbenchers and in the Lords, that HIV and Aids instruction would inevitably involve the teaching of homosexual practices and activity. To add to the controversy and confusion, a pamphlet produced by the Department for Education (DfE, as it was then), 'HIV and Aids: A Guide for the Education Service', was judged as being 'amoral' and 'judgement free' in the House of Lords, and criticised for 'explicitly describing oral sex' and 'deviant sexual practices' (Hansard, 5 March 1992, cols 977–8).

The Education Act 1993 (s. 241) went a step farther, making sex education part of the 'basic curriculum' to be provided by all maintained secondary schools. This was the first time sex education had ever been defined in law. The EA 1993 states that 'sex education' includes education about:

(a) Acquired Immune Deficiency Syndrome and Human Immunodeficiency Virus [i.e. Aids and HIV] and
(b) any other sexually transmitted disease (s. 241(2)(a)(b)).

However, owing to the concerns outlined above pertaining to proselytising about homosexual activity, the Act also introduced the requirement that the Secretary of State must amend the National Curriculum to exclude, from science, the study of HIV/Aids, sexually transmitted diseases (STDs) and any 'aspects of human behaviour, other than biological aspects' (s. 241(4)).

In summary, the Education Act 1993 stated that for all secondary-school-age children, sex education provision was compulsory. The schools must provide sex and relationship education (including HIV, Aids and STDs from September 1994). The biological aspects of human growth and reproduction should be taught through National Curriculum science. Parents were given the right to withdraw their child from receiving sex education, except that being delivered in the National Curriculum – that is the biological aspects provided in science classes (s. 241(3)).

Now, the 1944 Education Act and subsequently the Education Reform Act 1988 (s. 9(3)) gave parents the right to withdraw their children from religious education and collective worship. Similarly, the government's 'Sex and Relationship Guidance' (2000, s. 5.7) states that parents who choose to remove their children from sex and relationship education will be provided a standard pack of information given to the school by the DfEE. Oddly, then, the only people to whom the government provides detailed material about sex education are parents who decide that they do not want their children to partake in what the government offers!

The Education Act 1996 provides the current statute for sex education,[2] supplemented by the provisions of the Learning and Skills Act 2000. The latter Act states that the Secretary of State must issue guidance on the materials utilised to deliver sex education in schools, appropriate for the age, religious beliefs and culture of the pupils, who must be protected from inappropriate materials.

But the guidance circular 'Sex and Relationship Education Guidance' (DfEE, 0116/2000), which replaces the DfE Circular 5/94 'Sex Education in Schools' (1994), offers only anodyne comments on how children should be thus protected. Three distinct locations within the school timetable are identified here for the provision of sex education. First in the biology component of the National Curriculum for Science, second in the basic curriculum, and third via individual advice to pupils.[3] As we have noted, the Education Act 1993 stated that from September 1994 material on Aids, HIV, other sexually transmitted diseases, and non-biological aspects of human sexual behaviour were to be removed from the National Curriculum for Science. Prior to that, materials such as the Letts Study Guide *Science Single and Double Awards GCSE National Curriculum Key Stage 4* (Hill, 1993) had conveyed ideas such as the following:

> Aids stands for Acquired Immune Deficiency Syndrome. It is a virus. This virus attacks the immune system which protects the body against infections. Aids sufferers are therefore

---

2 The 1996 Act subsumed all previous education acts. The relevant sections from the 1993 Act are now s. 352(1)(c)(d), s. 352(3)(a)(b) and s. 356(9) respectively.

3 See Bridgeman, 1996: 45–69.

prone to illnesses, such as pneumonia and skin cancers, *which kill them*. It cannot be cured at the present time. (p. 93)

In 'Sex and Relationship Education Guidance' there is some consideration of the 'use of material' by teachers when presenting sex and relationship education:

Materials used in schools must be in accordance with the PSHE [Personal, Social and Health Education] framework and the law. Inappropriate images should not be used nor should explicit material not directly related to explanation ... Governors and head teachers should discuss with parents and take on board concerns raised, both on materials which are offered to schools and on sensitive material to be used in the classroom. The Department of Health will be issuing guidance to Health Authorities to make clear that any materials they develop for use in schools must be in line with this guidance ... (s. 1.8)

HIV and Aids are dealt with in sections 2.17–2.22. They are considered in conjunction with safer sex and sexually transmitted infections. Section 2.17 states that 'teaching about safer sex is one of the Government's key strategies for reducing the incidence of HIV/Aids and STIs [Sexually Transmitted Infections] ...' The 'Guidance' continues:

A survey conducted by National Opinion Poll (1996) indicated that young adults may be becoming complacent about the importance of safer sex, increasing their risk of infection and unwanted pregnancy or paternity. Strategies for teaching about HIV/Aids and STIs should include:
• Helping pupils clarify their knowledge of HIV/Aids and STIs;

- Teaching them assertiveness skills for negotiating relationships; and
- Enabling them to become effective users of services that help prevent/treat STIs and HIV. (s. 2.18)

Section 2.19 states that young people need to understand what constitutes 'risky behaviour'; they need to be given information and knowledge about 'HIV/Aids' and the use of a condom and safer sex in general. The taking of drugs and alcohol is mentioned in this section. In this context, however, the general message is that taking drugs and alcohol may lead to the loss of inhibitions and therefore lead to unprotected sex. The information that is lacking in this respect is that drug abuse lowers the immune system and is therefore an immune suppressant.

Importantly for the purposes of this paper, it is noted that the document treats HIV/Aids and STIs as though they are one and the same. STIs are mentioned in the same breath as HIV, implying that the risk of being infected with HIV is the same as being infected with STIs, and that they are equally common. (We shall see in Chapters 3 and 4 whether or not this can be sustained.) Section 2.20 states that the incidence of 'HIV/Aids infection remains unacceptably high for young men. Thirty-nine per cent of those with Aids in the UK are in their 20s, most of whom will have contracted HIV in their teens.' Again we note that omitted here is the statistical information concerning the ethnicity of those diagnosed with Aids, their country of *original* origin and their sexual orientation – issues again taken up in Chapter 3. What this guidance is alleging is that everyone is prone to the same risk of acquiring HIV.

There is a considerable amount of material available for Personal, Social and Health Education (PSHE), some of which relates to Aids and HIV. There are different forms of curriculum provision for PSHE. It can be provided through discrete curriculum time; teaching PSHE in and through other subjects/curriculum areas; through PSHE activities and school events; and through pastoral care and guidance. A non-statutory framework is given for PSHE in the National Curriculum, and teachers must use material published from other sources.

One such publication is *PASSPORT: A framework for personal and social development* (Lees and Plant, 2000), which seeks to initiate a process whereby schools can meet and plan PSD (Personal Social Development) requirements across the whole school curriculum. Under 'Learning outcomes' for Key Stage 3, the guide states that students should

> know about human reproduction, contraception, safe sexual practices, and the risks of early sexual activity. Know about HIV transmission and other sexually transmitted infections (STIs) and the associated high-risk behaviours.

For Key Stage 4, the learning outcomes include that students should

> Know the demographic trends in relation to STIs including HIV. Know the specific dangers of misusing alcohol and drugs in relation to: driving, pregnancy and sexually transmitted infections (STIs).

Once again HIV is mentioned in association with STIs, implying their similarity – again, an issue we take farther in Chapter 3.

Current state of play

The legislation now states that all schools must have an up-to-date sex and relationship education policy. It must be available for inspection and to parents. It must contain a definition of sex and relationship education, how this education is provided and by whom, how it is monitored and evaluated, and inform parents that their children may leave these lessons if parents deem this necessary. Governing bodies and head teachers must ensure that the sex and relationship education policy reflects both parents' wishes and the culture of the community the school serves.

Governing bodies of maintained primary schools must decide whether sex and relationship education should be included in their school's curriculum. They must determine what the educational provision consists of and how it should be organised. Maintained primary schools therefore have the option not to provide sex education. A written record must be kept whatever the governing body's decision. If it is decided that sex education should not be included, the statement must record this conclusion (Education (No. 2) Act 1986, s. 18). The school inspecting body, Ofsted (Office for Standards in Education), is statutorily required under Section 10 of the 'School Inspections Act' 1996 and the framework set in place in January 2000 to report on and evaluate the 'spiritual, moral, social and cultural development' of pupils in schools that are being inspected. It must comment upon and evaluate the school's sex and relationship education policy, and investigate and comment upon the involvement of parents with the construction of sex and relationship education policy.

All maintained secondary schools are statutorily required to provide sex and relationship education, including HIV and Aids and other sexually transmitted diseases. The teaching of human growth and reproduction must be delivered as set out in the National Curriculum. Sex education should be presented in a manner that encourages '... pupils to have due regard to moral considerations and family life' (EA 1996, s. 403(1)).

Summary

This chapter has explained the progression of sex and HIV and Aids education and its associated legal requirements since and before the 1988 ERA. Some of the literature available to schools to enable them to assemble a sex education and HIV/Aids programme has been investigated. What is quite apparent, however, is the lack of information for schools as to what the government would deem as 'appropriate' material and teaching methods with regard to HIV and Aids. Who can determine whether the information being delivered is 'accurate' or 'appropriate' when considering HIV and Aids? This provides a controversial and difficult area for those in the medical profession, let alone for teachers in secondary schools. These difficulties become very apparent as we move on to sample a few HIV and Aids lessons, as witnessed by researchers in schools in England.

2 SCHOOL PORTRAITS

Schools have to teach about HIV and Aids, but they have to access their information from many different sources and institutions. The governing bodies and head teachers together, in consultation with parents and teachers, may choose from an array of material. What sort of materials do they choose in practice, and how do they go about choosing?

Our research discovered material used by schools that had been developed by the following bodies:

- Health Education Authority
- AVERT (Aids Education & Research Trust)
- Tacade: educating for health
- (FPA) Family Planning Association
- Terrence Higgins Trust
- Brook Advisory Centres
- Sex Education Forum (National Children's Bureau)

How do schools make use of the range of material on offer? What follows is six sketches of lessons and episodes in schools and in local education authorities (LEAs), taken from class observations and interviews we carried out in six schools and two LEAs. The schools were selected randomly from a list of local schools, so what was happening in them is likely to be happening in similar schools around the country. We have no reason to believe that what we found is remarkable, or different from what is going on elsewhere, but of course the limited nature of the sample must be borne in mind in what follows. However, the intention of this chapter is to offer a glimpse into what was happening in some local schools, with the hope of stimulating further research and debate about the issue of HIV and Aids in schools more generally.

Throughout the following vignettes, where appropriate, we reference the source materials used by the teacher, as revealed in discussions with the teacher after the lessons had finished.

Six vignettes

First vignette

We visited one young but experienced Personal, Social and Health Education (PSHE) teacher in a local senior school, who used an array of materials to draw from for her lessons to a class of fourteen- to fifteen-year-olds. After they have settled down in the room, she tells the twenty or so students that this is one of their two lessons in the year concerning Aids and HIV. A few boys at the back of the room nudge each other and point at the girls, sniggering. The girls at the front looked uninterested. 'You're not going to talk about sex this early in the morning, are you, Miss?' asks one. The teacher continues undeterred. She hands out some leaflets and printed materials recounting some of the information delivered by the literature. 'It is estimated that there are 33.4 million people with HIV worldwide. Half of all new infections are now occurring among young people aged fifteen to twenty-four years,'[1] she reads. Pausing briefly to deal with some misbehaviour from the boys at the back, she then continues:

> On average, one person is infected every six hours in
> Britain.[2] This is a disease that can be described as an
> epidemic.[3] You can become infected by having vaginal or
> anal sex without a condom with someone who has HIV[4] or
> by injecting drugs using a needle or syringe, which has been
> used by an infected person. A mother can pass on the
> disease to her baby, before or after birth. HIV can also be
> passed on to the infant when the mother is breast feeding.
> There is no vaccine against HIV and there is no cure for HIV
> or Aids. The risk of infection is higher in some countries
> where more people are infected with HIV, but the risk of
> infection is everywhere. World wide, the commonest way of
> becoming infected with HIV is by sex between men and
> women.[5] The problem is you just can't tell who is infected
> with HIV as there are no outward signs.

The message conveyed to the students is that an HIV and Aids epidemic is sweeping the world. It is apparently a disease that cannot be cured. Even though the teacher is imparting all of this 'devastating' information, the pupils do not seem to be taking very much interest. A Martian visitor might be rather confused by the

---

1   Source: UNAids Report on the global HIV/Aids epidemic, December 1998, as stated in the Northumberland Health Authority leaflet 'How to be a Perfect Lover'.

2   'HIV & Aids: information for young people', a booklet produced by AVERT (Aids Education & Research Trust), 2000.

3   AVERT website: World HIV and Aids Statistics 'Summary of the HIV/Aids epidemic . . .' Source UNAids joint United Nations Programme on HIV/Aids, 'Aids epidemic update December 1999'.

4   'Lovelife: Sexual health for young people', a booklet produced by the Health Education Authority, 1999.

5   'Facts about Aids, HIV and the test', a booklet produced by the Health Education Authority, 1999.

students' apparent indifference to this 'epidemic' affecting every-one's life.

After reading from the leaflets and distributing copies for the students, the teacher moves on to the second, carefully orches-trated part of her lesson. She first lays pieces of paper on the floor with the numbers 1 to 10 written on them in large black marker pen. 'I'm going to take you on a journey,' she says, 'the time line journey of someone infected with HIV. I will walk along their life-line and show you how HIV will develop through their life and how this person, unknowingly, spreads the disease to others in the community.' Our Martian visitor might here note that the teacher possesses the air and authority of a doctor or a nurse, and would be perhaps surprised to hear afterwards that in fact she is basing all this information on some fact sheets she has picked up on the World Wide Web. She continues:

> Here I am at the beginning of my time line. I have slept with
> my boyfriend having unprotected sex as I am on the pill.
> Unfortunately I don't know all of my boyfriend's partners
> and one of them has the HIV virus. You see, you just can't
> tell if someone is HIV, because for years they look normal.

The teacher starts jumping from one piece of paper to another:

> I have many boyfriends over the years. I have unprotected
> sex with all of them, and so I am infecting them with HIV.

The teacher steps more rapidly onto the other pieces of paper.

> Around year nine I start feeling unwell, and because my
> immune system is damaged by HIV I develop skin cancer
> and other diseases such as tuberculosis and pneumonia.

As the teacher steps onto the last piece of paper, number 10, she falls into a heap on the floor.

The school bell rings at this point. The children all stand up, pick up their books, and walk out of the room chatting and laughing with each other, seemingly unfazed by it all.

Second vignette

We visited the Advisory Teacher for Health Issues in one local education authority. He told us about the various sources that schools could use to gather and obtain their information on HIV and Aids: 'From published resources, from the FPA, or Sex Education Forum, or from literature published in science books, such as microbiology, or information found on the Internet.' He told us 'it is up to the individual school and teacher to make up their mind as to which publications to utilise in their HIV and Aids lessons'. However, when we raised doubts here, he reassured us that 'Anything that has been published must have had to go through some sort of rigorous publishing procedure, mustn't it? So the information given by a published article must be correct.'

He is there to advise, but ultimately, he told us,

> teachers use their own skills to decide upon the information they wish to use and deliver in their lessons. AVERT, and the Terrence Higgins Trust, are experts in the field of HIV and Aids; if they have material available then this would be fine to use in school lessons. Credible people write these booklets with a reputation for HIV and Aids knowledge, especially the Terrence Higgins Trust.

Furthermore, he informed us that

> Young people can pick up information and leaflets from our

local health authority advisory clinics as well as from school. The children can obtain brochures pertaining to all kinds of health issues, including HIV, and attend a health clinic specifically for young people.

He had to hand some of the leaflets that were available in the local health clinic for children who called by, as he suggested teachers advise students to do. They included 'Gay Men and Safer Sex', produced in 1996 by the Health Education Authority, and 'Young Gay Men: a guide to coming out', produced in 1994 by the Terrence Higgins Trust. The adviser seemed blissfully unaware of any contentious issues contained within these leaflets. Nor did he seem at all perturbed by the language used in these pamphlets to describe acceptable behaviour.

Readers can judge for themselves. Here are a couple of quotes from this material – and we warn those who may be offended by explicit discussion to skip quickly to the next vignette. But as what we are quoting is material being recommended by at least one advisory teacher in a local education authority for use in compulsory Aids and HIV education with students aged from eleven to sixteen, it seems worth spelling out some details.

First, the Terrence Higgins Trust publication states:

... What you do in bed is limited only by imagination. Some men wank each other off, others suck each other's dicks, while others like fucking.
... Most types of gay sex are quite safe. To get infected with HIV ... you need to get the blood or cum of someone who is infected into your bloodstream. So things like kissing and wanking are safe ... the main risk comes from fucking without a condom, as the virus can get down the opening of your cock or through the lining of your arse ...

Second, the Health Education Authority leaflet states:

> ... Tonguing your partner's anus (rimming): there's little risk of giving or getting HIV by rimming – as long as no blood gets into the mouth or anus. But you can get other infections like hepatitis B this way ... Fingering and fisting: the risk of passing on HIV by fingering and fisting is low. Try not to tear or damage the inside of the anus. Keep fingernails trimmed and smooth. For fisting, use a latex glove and plenty of lubricant. Even so, fisting can still cause tears inside the anus ...

Third vignette

We visited a staffroom in one of the local secondary schools, sitting next to the PSHE teacher, who was sipping a cup of coffee and talking to a colleague. At this school, it is the form teachers – those whose responsibilities include taking the register and checking on absenteeism – who have, apparently for the first time, been given the task of sex and HIV/Aids education. The head teacher believes that this will provide a bond between the teacher and their year group. These form teachers have no experience of or training in delivering such information. The head of PSHE, who had previously been responsible for sex and HIV and Aids lessons, has had to provide the form teachers with leaflets and lesson plans to help them with their treatment of the subject. HIV and Aids lessons are to take place during the morning form period. Many of the form teachers have stated that they do not feel comfortable with the idea or qualified to teach the subject and, because of their wariness and reluctance, the PSHE teacher thinks that in some tutor groups the subject may not be taught at all.

'I don't utilise statistics or demographic analysis in my HIV and Aids lessons,' the PSHE teacher informs her colleague.

> I just don't have the time to gather the data or keep it up to date. I teach HIV and Aids along with other STDs. Information from the Terrence Higgins Trust and the Health Education Authority is all very useful. Mind you, we get so much stuff in the post, you can only take so much of it in. Information comes from all sorts of people who have received grants, winning them on the condition that they provide some educational blurb for us in schools. But you must be careful about talking to the children about the crisis in Africa or using the situation there as an example of HIV and Aids. The children would only say that those in Africa started the disease so they 'deserve all that they get'. The messages you need to get across to the kids are to practise safe sex to protect against HIV and Aids, that all groups are at the same risk of contracting HIV, and that HIV always transforms into Aids which is a disease from which you die.

'The children no longer consider HIV or Aids to be a homosexual disease, then?' asks the other teacher. 'No, that association has long been forgotten,' replies the PSHE teacher. 'Good,' says the other teacher.

Fourth vignette

Some schools choose to teach the subject of HIV and Aids through a cross-curriculum perspective. One such school we were lucky to visit during 'World Aids Week'. Throughout the school, posters and artwork were displayed. The headmaster proudly showed us all their activities.

'This "World Aids Week" is allowing our students to become

generally aware of health issues relating to HIV and Aids, don't you know?' the headmaster expounded, as he strode across the playground with the researcher.

> I am very proud of our children. They have organised a profusion of activities, from the 'design an Aids T-shirt competition', to the 'HIV and Aids poster and leaflet writing award', and they have been participating on the local health authority web page. The children hope to raise over £2,000 for Aids charities. Yes, yes, we all must do our bit, don't you know. In the dinner-times the sixth-form students have been distributing Aids helpline numbers to younger members of the school. One's peers are always good at providing information for other members of our school, don't you find?

Two children, aged about fifteen, are playing a card game called 'High Risk – Low Risk' on a bench. Cards printed with certain phrases are placed on the bench. The children decide whether the card represents an activity that has a 'high'- or a 'low'-risk association with becoming infected with HIV. Phrases on the cards include 'intercourse without a condom', 'dental treatment', 'deep kissing', 'blood transfusion', and so it goes on. The friends are in conversation with each other as the headmaster and researcher stand, listening, to one side: 'Remember: everyone with HIV is someone's brother, sister, mother, father, husband, wife or child. Our teacher told us how you get HIV. You can get it having sex with a man or a woman.' The friend nods. 'Or you can catch it through sharing syringes when you inject drugs or through transfusions of infected blood or blood products. She also said your mum can give it to you when you are born.' 'And when you are a baby ... ' So the conversation continues as the headmaster leads the researcher back to his office.

Fifth vignette

The teacher in charge of health education is sitting in the staffroom of a primary school where HIV and Aids education is optional. She carries on a conversation with other members of staff and the researchers.

> We don't have to tell the children about HIV, it really isn't topical at the moment anyway. In 'Circle Time' we deal with issues that the children raise and usually they are related to subjects they see on the television, so HIV and Aids isn't one that comes up. If it did, I would tell the children that it is a disease, caused by a virus, and that they should be aware that if they see any discarded hypodermic needles they should not pick them up, as you could catch HIV by pricking yourself with the dirty needle. The only time the HIV and Aids issue is raised really is with the dinner ladies ... we always tell them to wear gloves when treating nose bleeds ... but ... well ... sometimes they don't, but we have told them. It's for their own safety. That's why when a child is sick or wets itself we like the children to clear it up as much as they can themselves ...

Sixth vignette

The following is a snippet from a conversation with a head of Personal, Social and Health Education who teaches sex education to fourteen-, fifteen- and sixteen-year-olds. She tells the researcher that one scenario she utilises in her lessons, to stimulate discussion, is the potential arrival of an HIV-positive child at the school.

> The children are very good when discussing and dealing with this situation. I can safely say that all of them would welcome the child into the school and offer them support

and try to help them in any way possible. But, you know, what is really alarming is that I discussed this 'case study' with the teachers who are taking over the HIV and Aids education programme in the school from the beginning of term. When I mentioned the case study, of the HIV-positive child coming to the school, the teachers were totally shocked. They stated that they would want to know how the child had become infected, just in case we could all be at risk from their disease. They said they would all be against admitting the child to our school. They felt that parents and governors would also concur with this view.

Five propositions

The six vignettes here present a flavour of what is likely to be going on under the name of HIV and Aids education in secondary and primary schools around the country. They also give a sense of the material young people are being presented with, and how they are responding to it.

Figure 1 **Five propositions showing how HIV and Aids are taught in schools**

1. All are at the same risk of becoming HIV seropositive – heterosexual and homosexual, drug users and non-drug users;

2. Those testing HIV seropositive always proceed to develop Aids;

3. HIV seropositivity progresses to Aids at the same rate for all risk groups – so, in particular, heterosexual non-drug users from the UK have the same chance of becoming HIV seropositive and progressing to Aids as any other group;

4. HIV is in all relevant respects the same as other sexually transmitted infections;

5. HIV and Aids are significant health risks, more significant (because education about them is compulsory in schools) than other health and safety risks.

We can summarise the views taken on HIV and Aids in the lessons we saw, the conversations we had with teachers and advisers, and in looking through the material, in the five propositions in Figure 1.

It is our suggestion that these five propositions will inform much of what goes on in Aids and HIV education around the country. Certainly they also seem to inform much of the popular media discussion about Aids and HIV. In the next chapter we turn to look at some of the evidence, to examine whether or not what is being taught in schools coincides with the reality as science finds it.

3 HIV AND AIDS: THE EVIDENCE

The origins of Aids

Aids was reported as a new medical syndrome in 1981 in New York City, Los Angeles and San Francisco. It immediately attracted the attention of not only clinical and public health experts, but also the broader general public. It continued to gain media focus when well-known celebrities died and were associated with this new phenomenon, Aids. Why? Because it was a new disease, its cause was unknown, it was incurable, it seemed to be fatal ... and because it occurred exclusively in homosexual men and drug addicts. Further spread was confined to these groups.[1]

When a similar disease was reported in haemophiliac men and in some other persons who had received transfusions of blood or blood products, transmission of a blood-borne infection was also suspected. This view was supported when, in 1983, a new agent (a retrovirus) was reported.[2] This was later named the Human Immune-deficiency Virus (HIV), and presumed then to be the

---

1 It was supposed that the illness in these people was due to an infectious agent transmitted by anal intercourse between men and/or by the sharing of contaminated needles by users of intravenous drugs.

2 It was found in complex cell cultures inoculated with material from an enlarged lymph gland excised from an otherwise well homosexual man in Paris (Barre-Sinoussi et al., 1983). An identical agent was then reported as having been isolated from the blood of homosexual men in the USA (Zagury et al., 1984).

cause of Aids. Subsequently, HIV was allegedly found also in sexual secretions and in the blood of persons with Aids, and it was assumed therefore that it would spread to general populations by heterosexual transmission. Since there were at that time no prospects of drugs or vaccines for prevention or cure, it was concluded that the outbreak of Aids in the USA would spread as an epidemic to other countries and eventually become a pandemic with millions of cases worldwide in the 1990s (Anderson et al. 1989). However, no such epidemic occurred in the UK (Stewart, 1993, 1995) or in the industrialised countries of Europe and Australasia where Aids remains confined to the original high-risk groups.

Two points of clarification

HIV seropositive and HIV positive

There is much ignorance and confusion about just what is meant by having Aids[3] and being HIV 'positive', the usual term used in schools and popular debates. Some of this confusion we hope to clear up as we proceed through this chapter. However, two points are worth clarifying at the outset. First, we will, somewhat pedantically, continue to refer to HIV 'seropositivity' throughout, rather than the more commonly used expression HIV 'positive'. This is because the vast majority of tests for HIV, such as Elisa and Western Blot, are *indirect* in that they generally detect antibodies, not

---

3   Aids is one of several headings which may be legitimately used under HIV Disease in the ICD 942-044, with or without Aids-defining or other additional detail in morbidity and mortality records. Persons who are seropositive but without symptoms can be classified as HIV Disease in morbidity statistics.

the virus itself. Hence the tests detect antibodies in the serum rather than the virus itself. If the antibodies are detected the presence of the virus is assumed. Hence the term HIV seropositive is strictly more accurate than the term HIV positive, and, as will be seen, it pays to be precise in these often fraught and controversial discussions.[4]

What is Aids?

Second, it is worth being clear at the outset precisely what we mean by Aids. Aids is *not* a single new disease, as is generally supposed. An individual suffering from Aids could be afflicted by any one of about 26 long-established and well-known diseases, such as tuberculosis and enteritis. It is only in the presence of HIV seropositivity that tuberculosis, for example, ceases to be tuberculosis and becomes classed as Aids. Hence a person with tuberculosis who has *not* been tested for HIV antibodies or who has tested *negative* should be classed as having tuberculosis, not Aids. The importance of this point will also become apparent as we proceed through the discussion in this and the next chapter.

Who is at risk of becoming HIV seropositive?

We now turn to the first of our five propositions which we left hanging at the end of Chapter 2, and which seemed to be informing Aids and HIV education in schools, viz.:

- All are at the same risk of becoming HIV seropositive –

---

4   See Chapter 4 for further elaboration of the importance of this point.

heterosexual and homosexual, drug users and non-drug users.

How does this first proposition bear up under scrutiny?

From a few dozen cases in 1981, Aids increased in 2000 to a cumulative total of over 750,000 registered cases in the USA (US Department of Health and Human Services, 2000), 17,209 in the UK and many thousands or tens of thousands elsewhere. Since 1994, there has been a clear downward trend in the number of new cases and deaths (Table 1).

By 2000 in the USA, Britain and countries of northern Europe, the majority of cases still occurred in male homosexuals and, with decreasing incidence, in drug users of both sexes. There has, however, been a small but steady increase of new cases in females who are sexual partners of bisexual men or who engage in anal intercourse, other forms of high-risk sexual activity, or seek sexual experiences abroad.

While there are currently fewer than 500 deaths (and falling) from Aids per year, the chances of dying from other causes are much higher. Six times more people are killed in motor vehicle accidents every year than die of Aids. As discussed below, every year about as many people die from Aids as die from falling down the stairs in the home.

Current figures of HIV seropositivity are shown in Table 2 (see p. 49). This shows that positive tests for HIV seropositivity (that is HIV 'positive') continue to rise in all regions in the UK with the exceptions of the south-east of England (excluding London), northern England and Yorkshire, and Scotland.

Meanwhile, the frequency of sexually transmitted infections (STIs) such as gonorrhoea, chlamydia and others is showing an

Table 1 **UK Aids cases by year of diagnosis and death in HIV-seropositive individuals by year of death**

Year	Aids diagnoses	Known deaths[1]	Aids deaths[2]	Total deaths
1984 or earlier	161	160	69	89
1985	247	239	121	152
1986	474	468	270	320
1987	681	653	352	417
1988	908	865	413	482
1989	1,082	1,036	667	744
1990	1,244	1,107	788	895
1991	1,387	1,216	995	1,106
1992	1,578	1,347	1,094	1,236
1993	1,785	1,460	1,358	1,563
1994	1,851	1,327	1,533	1,700
1995	1,764	978	1,514	1,718
1996	1,425	524	1,235	1,460
1997	1,064	289	564	735
1998	767	196	346	505
1999	715	177	305	459
2000	718	122	263	413
Unknown	0	0	222	245
Total	17,851	12,164	12,109	14,239[3]

Source: www.phls.co.uk/facts/HIV/hivqnotes.htm (25/10/01)

1 Number of those in the previous column whose deaths were reported by the end of June 2001.

2 By year death occurred.

3 Includes 150 Aids cases lost to follow-up who are presumed to have died.

unprecedented increase, leading to a rapid rise in total incidence between 1995 and the end of 1999. Outside London and localised foci in Brighton, Edinburgh and Dundee, Aids is a rare disease in the UK, but the connection with overseas locations and partners remains. This situation is an obvious target for prevention which has been largely obscured by official policies which insist on protecting those testing HIV seropositive at the expense of those at risk, who include wives, partners, unborn infants, neonates and others. These are uncounted, and the system adopted by those responsible for public health in the UK has made them uncountable. Thus the immense medical, social and economic problems associated with Aids and related diseases will continue. In the meantime the true incidence, as assessed by clinical cases in the main risk groups, including immigrants and those who acquire disease abroad, is also guaranteed to continue.[5]

In 1999 there were 1,321 new cases of low-risk heterosexually acquired HIV seropositivity in the UK.[6] Of these, 114 cases (8.6 per cent) were acquired in the UK from partners infected outside the UK. Another 1,089 (82.4 per cent) acquired their infection abroad and of these 908 (68.7 per cent) in Africa. Coincidentally, another 114 cases were under investigation and 4 cases closed with no further information available. In other words 91 per cent of low-risk heterosexually acquired HIV seropositivity was either the result of exposure to individuals from abroad or of unexplained non-specific reactions or other diseases.

All of this leads to the firm conclusion that Aids, in Britain, the United States and northern Europe, is a compendium of loosely classified diseases which increased at first exclusively in the original high-risk groups (HRG): homosexual and bisexual men, drug addicts and women who are partners of men in these

---

5   This has been exacerbated by the decision in 1998 to regard all seropositives as cases of Aids or Aids-related complex (ARCs) even when they are asymptomatic, unidentified and untraceable. They remain therefore on the cumulative register and increase in proportion to the numbers tested, which is an open option for expansion on all fronts, including the influence and financing of those who manipulate the option.

6   Numbers of HIV and Aids are reclassified over time as further reports are received. Hence for most recent years, some figures may be inconsistent.

Table 2 HIV seropositive individuals by country, region and year of HIV seropositive diagnosis

Country and region of diagnosis	1984 or earlier	1986	1990	1992	1994	1996	1998	1999	Total	% change 1986–99
ENGLAND Northern & Yorkshire	66	118	90	103	83	90	77	97	1,474	− 17.8
North-west	72	148	141	170	140	176	173	187	2,460	+ 26.3
Trent	2	70	71	83	69	72	80	76	1,132	+ 8.5
West Midlands	61	65	88	83	75	58	106	89	1,332	+ 36.9
Eastern	19	82	52	90	60	54	85	89	1,124	+ 8.5
London	773	1,619	1,627	1,688	1,567	1,694	1,742	1,871	25,983	+15.5
South-east	50	242	196	229	233	225	206	218	3,464	− 9.9
South-west	39	80	97	83	106	76	99	96	1,380	+ 20.0
ENGLAND (total)	1,212	2,424	2,362	2,529	2,333	2,445	2,568	2,723	38,349	+ 12.3
WALES	39	32	36	50	44	36	29	33	612	+ 3.1
N. IRELAND	1	12	12	12	14	16	9	13	197	+ 8.3
SCOTLAND	349	296	119	130	141	157	146	139	2,907	− 53.0
UK TOTAL	1,611	2,764	2,529	2,721	2,532	2,654	2,752	2,908	42,065	+ 5.2
Channel Isles/ Isle of Man	1	2	3	1	8	6	5	1	60	− 50.0

Source: www.phls.co.uk/facts/HIV/hivqnotes.htm (21/11/00)
1 Individuals with laboratory reports of infection plus those with Aids or death reports for whom no matching laboratory report has been received.

Table 3 **Estimated risk of becoming HIV seropositive**

	One sexual encounter	*500 sexual encounters*
Partner never tested		
Not in high-risk group		
Using condoms	1 in 50,000,000	1 in 110,000
Not using condoms	1 in 5,000,000	1 in 16,000
High-risk groups (HRG)		
Using condoms	1 in 100,000 to 1 in 10,000	1 in 210 to 1 in 21
Not using condoms	1 in 10,000 to 1 in 1,000	1 in 32 to 1 in 3
Partner tested negative		
No history of HRB[1]		
Using condoms	1 in 5,000,000,000	1 in 11,000,000
Not using condoms	1 in 500,000,000	
Continuing HRB		
Using condoms	1 in 500,000	
Not using condoms	1 in 50,000	
Partner tested seropositive		
Using condoms	1 in 5,000	
Not using condoms	1 in 500	

Source: Hearst and Hulley, 1988
1 HRB – high-risk behaviour.

categories. The feared spread to the general population outside of these risk groups *is so low as to be negligible* in its impact on the resident population of the UK and therefore on health statistics and cost.

Epidemiological calculations bear out this phenomenon, as shown in Table 3.

These figures indicate quite clearly why HIV seropositivity has remained within the original high-risk groups. Where a man or woman has not been tested for HIV antibodies, and does not belong to a high-risk group, the chance of contracting HIV antibodies from a single unprotected sexual encounter is in the order of 1 in 5,000,000. It is not surprising, therefore, that there are so few documented cases in the medical research literature of becoming HIV seropositive after a single heterosexual encounter. Even taking the worst case, where a person has a single heterosexual encounter with a partner who has tested seropositive for HIV, the chances of infection are 1 in 500. Even if that person had a heterosexual encounter with an HIV-seropositive person every day for a year, the chance (conditional probability = $\{1 - [499/500]^{365}\}$ = 0.482) of becoming HIV seropositive falls to about 1 in 2.[7]

In response to these figures, critics argue that most individuals do not know what their partner's HIV seropositive status is or whether they belong to a high-risk group, and that the figures therefore give a false sense of security. HIV seropositivity is a marker for individuals who engage in high-risk activity and associate with others within defined social groupings and lifestyles. So whilst injecting drug users are likely to socialise with other injecting drug users, non-drug users tend not to socialise with users. As we have seen, in schools, Aids and HIV are treated as if they are just like any other sexually transmitted infections (STIs); that is, as diseases which are similarly infectious. It could be argued, therefore, that sex education has been vicariously successful in preventing heterosexual spread of the virus where there is little or no risk, although unsuccessful in preventing transmission in those most at risk. However, as we shall see below, it would be incorrect to argue this because the spread of other sexually transmitted diseases in the heterosexual population, and especially among young people, is increasing rapidly.

---

7   These risk estimates are also supported by important studies carried out over a long period; see, for example, Padian et al., 1990.

So, to return to our first proposition ('All are at the same risk of becoming HIV seropositive – heterosexual and homosexual, drug users and non-drug users'), there seems to be enough evidence to challenge this unequivocally:

Question: Is everyone at the same risk of becoming HIV seropositive?

Answer: No. Not everyone is at the same risk of becoming HIV seropositive and of contracting Aids. Those at risk, in Britain, the United States and northern Europe, are more likely to hail from high-risk groups (HRGs): homosexual and bisexual men; drug addicts; women who are partners of men in these categories or those who engage in sexual activities with partners from high-Aids-incidence countries.

Does HIV seropositivity always progress to Aids?

We now turn to the second and third of our stated propositions that seem to inform the way HIV and Aids are taught in schools, viz.:

- Those testing HIV seropositive always proceed to develop Aids;
- HIV seropositivity progresses to Aids at the same rate for all risk groups – so, in particular, heterosexual non-drug users from the UK have the same chance of becoming HIV seropositive and progressing to Aids as any other group;

What does the available evidence say about these propositions? Current public expenditure on the syndrome is predicated on the assumption that all HIV seropositivity will lead to Aids and death. If this is so, the current decline in Aids deaths and diagnoses may only be temporary.

Now, because of the insistence on confidentiality and anonymity in surveys in the UK and USA, details about those testing HIV seropositive but not progressing to Aids are difficult or impossible to obtain. However, there is clear circumstantial evidence to support the notion that the great majority of those diagnosed as HIV seropositive do not go on to develop Aids.[8]

First, there is evidence from Scotland. A working party (Scottish Home and Health Department, 1993, 1996) estimated that there were 5,000 individuals testing HIV seropositive in 1989.

---

8   A comprehensive, anonymised surveillance for seroprevalence of HIV was conducted throughout the UK in 1998 (Department of Health, 1999). A total of 649,076 specimens were obtained from 240 centres or districts dealing with genito-urinary medicine (GUM), drug users and pregnant women. The sample was to some extent biased in that the patients attending the GU clinics were obviously in a risk category, difficult to quantify since GUM now includes all STIs (STD is now a non-term). The overall prevalence in homosexual men in this group was 8.4 per cent, a decline from 22 per cent in 1990 and 19 per cent in 1993, that is about 15 per cent per year, with an excess at all ages and all stages in London. This, however, is linked to risk behaviour which gives homosexual men over 20 per cent of all gonorrhoea and a high frequency of hepatitis B and C. There is a high progression to Aids in this group, probably over 50 per cent, with much lower frequencies in the other groups. This is influenced by location and country of origin. Women from Africa attending antenatal clinics in London show a high prevalence of seropositivity and account for most of the perinatal transmission. Matching this, 87 per cent of cases in London were acquired by presumed heterosexual transmission abroad, largely in Africa. Clinical progression and secondary attack rates from these sources are not known because anonymous surveys do not provide the opportunity for follow-up or for partner information or notification. In this respect, HIV/Aids enjoys a confidentiality and privileged status not accorded to any other disease.

They predicted[9] that there would be 1,100 cases[10] requiring care in Strathclyde and Lothian in 1993, plus 1,800 cases elsewhere in Scotland.[11] They estimated that this would lead to a cumulative total of 950–1,200 with Aids in 1996, and used the prediction to emphasise the danger of heterosexual transmission of HIV antibodies. But the actual total in 1996 turned out to be 825 cases. The working party then predicted that there would be 280–350 new cases of Aids in 1995, but the actual total was 115, falling to 83 in 1996, 38 in 1998 and 32 in 1999. *Obviously the majority of HIV seropositives were not progressing to Aids.*

Second, in the UK, with over 42,000 HIV seropositives already identified cumulatively, total diagnoses for Aids fell from 1,425 in 1996 to 1,064, to 767 and to 715 in the succeeding years to 1999. The most significant statistic is the cumulative total of only 18,000 cases of Aids in the UK from 1982 to 2000. Almost this entire number is in the original risk groups, including immigrants, with a diminishing number of new registrations of Aids. This figure would be very much higher if all HIV seropositives or contacts went on to develop Aids. Again, clearly the majority of HIV seropositives are not progressing to Aids.

Third, in the USA there has been follow-up of sample populations, including hundreds of thousands of recruits to the armed forces. Despite having a steady frequency of HIV seropositivity of 1/250 (0.4 per cent) since 1984 (Duesberg, 1996), Aids first increased and *then declined in incidence*. The proportion which is HIV

---

9   Using CD4 lymphocyte counts as an immunological marker. Counts of CD4 lymphocytes are not required in the UK for diagnosis or monitoring. They are recognised under ICD 042-044 in the USA and some other countries.

10   Confidence limits 750–8,700.

11   With CD4 counts of less than 200, i.e. also progressing to Aids.

seropositive has remained stable, yet there are no reports of spontaneous outbreaks of Aids among them. Clearly something other than testing seropositive for HIV leads to progression to Aids – and these other factors are likely to be the risk behaviour of those affected.

So, what about the second and third propositions? Again, they would seem to have unequivocal answers.

Question: Do those testing HIV seropositive always proceed to develop Aids?

Answer: No. A person who tests seropositive for HIV may not go on to develop Aids. Progression and speed of progression to Aids depend less upon testing HIV seropositive than upon the risk behaviour of those affected.

Question: Does HIV seropositivity progress to Aids at the same rate for all risk groups? Do heterosexual non-drug users in the UK have the same chance of becoming HIV seropositive progressing to Aids as any other group?

Answer: No. Progression to Aids may be swift and afflict 100 per cent in partners of promiscuous homosexual men. By comparison there may be *zero* progression in those who, although HIV seropositive, do not engage in risk behaviour. For instance, many of the spouses of haemophiliac men can now be identified in good health fifteen years after first detection of their HIV seropositive state. Thus it appears that there is no risk of progression to Aids even though some people test HIV seropositive. Intermediate rates (and speed of progression to Aids) of 10–50 per cent occur in drug addicts and others. The time period that exists between becoming HIV seropositive and the development of one of the diseases classified as Aids and death is different for each individual.

HIV, Aids and sexually transmitted infections (STIs)

We turn to our fourth proposition, viz.:

- HIV is in all relevant respects the same as other sexually transmitted infections.

The evidence seems not to support this either. First, HIV antibodies can be transmitted in ways other than sexual intercourse: from mother to child; by blood transfusion; by injection from a contaminated needle. In this respect HIV and Aids are different from sexually transmitted infections.

Individuals are only at risk of becoming HIV seropositive during high-risk sexual intercourse; that is if they are homosexual, sexually active with a partner who is bisexual, a drug user, perform anal sex, or are from a country with a high incidence of Aids. In other words only those indulging in these high-risk activities are putting themselves at risk of becoming HIV seropositive and possibly developing Aids.

By comparison the incidence of common STIs such as gonorrhoea, HSV (herpes), chlamydia and others is showing unprecedented increases, because *all are at risk.* There is therefore a clear distinction between HIV and Aids and other STIs. Other sexually transmitted diseases and infections are associated with all members of the community, not just those in certain high-risk groups.

Table 4 shows the number of cases in England of five sexually transmitted diseases over the period 1995–9. First, diagnoses of gonorrhoea in England have risen steadily from 9,962 to 15,572; a total rise of 56 per cent. Rises occurred across most age groups but were particularly large in teenagers (84.4 per cent). Second, diagnoses of genital warts in males aged less than 20 years increased by

Table 4 **Sexually transmitted infections diagnosed in GUM clinics (England)**

	1995	1996	1997	1998	1999	% change
Gonorrhoea, total	9,962	11,929	12,462	12,501	15,572	+ 56.3
Male homosexually acquired <20	32	53	80	53	86	+ 168.8
< 20 yrs male	717	917	1,094	1,023	1,415	+ 97.3
< 20 yrs female	1,131	1,517	1,577	1,631	1,992	+ 76.1
All < 20 yrs	1,848	2,434	2,671	2,654	3,407	+ 84.4
Genital warts, total	51,289	54,652	58,816	59,727	61,559	+ 20.0
All male homosexually acquired	1,331	1,274	1,474	1,507	1,585	+ 19.1
< 20 yrs male	1,805	2,047	2,472	2,788	3,095	+ 71.4
< 20 yrs female	6,884	7,780	8,361	8,659	8,637	+ 25.5
All < 20 yrs	8,689	9,827	10,833	11,447	11,732	+ 35.0
Genital herpes, total	15,044	15,192	15,130	15,671	15,863	+ 5.4
All male homosexually acquired	324	384	334	302	335	+ 3.4
< 20 yrs male	282	270	265	324	346	+ 22.7
< 20 yrs female	1,699	1,715	1,856	1,880	1,949	+ 14.7
All < 20 yrs	1,981	1,985	2,121	2,204	2,295	+ 15.9
Chlamydia, total	29,286	32,521	38,997	44,089	51,083	+ 74.4
All male homosexually acquired	227	279	353	455	612	+ 169.6
< 20 yrs male	1,184	1,402	1,852	2,401	2,958	+ 149.8
< 20 yrs female	5,100	6,128	7,818	8,844	10,638	+ 108.6
All < 20 yrs	6,284	7,530	9,670	11,245	13,596	+ 116.3
All STIs acquired homosexually	3,268	3,644	3,959	3,969	4,414	+ 35.1
Homosexually acquired STIs in London	2,005	2,177	2,235	2,224	2,493	+ 24.3
% of total	61.3	59.7	56.5	56.0	56.5	
All STIs < 20 yrs males	3,991	4,641	5,686	6,541	7,819	+ 95.9
All STIs < 20 yrs females	14,816	17,146	19,615	21,017	23,227	+ 56.8

Source: www.phls.co.uk/facts/STI/DataOnSTIsInEng9599.htm (21/11/00)

71 per cent, and there was a similar pattern in females, where cases rose by 25 per cent. Third, although the number of new diagnoses of genital herpes in England changed little (15,044 to 15,863, a rise of 5.4 per cent), diagnoses among teenage males and females rose by 15.9 per cent. Fourth, the number of diagnoses of genital chlamydia in England increased dramatically by 74.4 per cent from 29,286 to 51,083. The rise occurred in all regions and in both sexes and in all age groups but was particularly sharp in males and females under 20 years of age where the number of diagnoses increased by 116.3 per cent. Fifth, diagnoses of infectious syphilis in England rose, from a relatively low base, by 56 per cent (from 132 to 206). Most of this rise was seen in men, where the number of cases rose from 102 to 152. Most changes in reported cases occur where there are local outbreaks of syphilis in homosexual men.

Even on their own, the figures in this table demonstrate an unambiguous failure and a damning indictment of sex education in schools – but there is more bad news to come.

If even the 'wear a condom' message on Aids and HIV sex education in schools were successful, we would not only be expecting a decline in sexually transmitted diseases but also a decline in the number of conceptions and unwanted pregnancies among young people. Table 5 shows that for England, over the last ten years, while there has been a fall of 6.1 per cent in the number of conceptions to women of all ages and a fall of 7.2 per cent to women under 20 years, there has been a small rise in the number of conceptions to women under 16 years. There has been no change in the percentage of conceptions being aborted. The UK has the highest teenage pregnancy rate in Europe; in England there were 97,600 conceptions in 1997 ('Teenage Pregnancy', Cm. 4342, June 1999, Figure 2). Of these about 37,290 were aborted. These remaining

Table 5 **Fertility: conceptions and abortions (England)**

	1991	1992	1993	1994	1995	1996	1997	%
Conceptions (000)								
All ages	809.1	784.9	776.8	760.4	749.9	774.5	759.5	− 6.1
Under 20	96.9	87.7	81.7	80	81.1	88.8	89.9	− 7.2
Under 16	7.4	6.7	6.8	7.3	7.5	8.2	7.7	+ 4.1
Rate per 000								
All ages	77.8	76.4	76.3	74.8	73.8	76.1	74.5	
Under 20	64.8	61.7	59.6	58.6	58.5	62.9	62.2	
Under 16	9.3	8.3	8.0	8.3	8.5	9.3	8.8	
Percentage terminated by abortion								
All ages	19.5	19.5	19.3	19.6	19.9	21.0	21.5	
Under 20	34.8	34.2	34.6	35.1	35.1	36.7	37.2	
Under 16	51.1	48.8	50.4	50.6	48	49.6	50.1	

Source: www.doh.gov.uk/hpsss/tbl_A13.htm (21/11/00)

live birth rates for teenagers compare very unfavourably with figures reported for the Netherlands, Ireland, Germany, France and Italy (ibid., Figure 3).

The main conclusion to be drawn from these figures is that sex education is failing comprehensively and with no evidence of correction. There is, however, a positive lesson in that the figures reveal the difference between groups in terms of age, sex, behaviour and location. This should provide, from now on, a basis for a more effective strategy.

Question: Is HIV in all relevant respects the same as other sexually transmitted infections, and should it be taught in schools as if it were?
Answer: No. HIV and Aids are quite distinct from other sexually transmitted infections. It is possible to become HIV seropositive

through activities other than sexual contact. Unlike common sexually transmitted diseases, not everyone is at the same risk of becoming HIV seropositive and possibly developing Aids. There are high-risk groups and low-risk groups. There are high-risk activities and low-risk activities. Individuals avoiding high-risk behaviour will avoid becoming HIV seropositive.

HIV and Aids as significant health risks

Our final proposition states that:

- HIV and Aids are significant health risks, more significant than other health and safety risks.

The fact that the teaching of HIV and Aids is compulsory in schools would suggest an imperative need to warn youngsters of the threat to their wellbeing constituted by the disease. HIV and Aids must therefore be considered a significant health risk, presumably more so than other diseases and health-threatening situations.

However, Table 6 above calls this proposition into question. It would seem on the face of it that there are many other candidates in terms of diseases and dangers to health that it would be more beneficial for children to learn about in school. These diseases and life-threatening situations are much more likely to claim or form part of the lives of those currently learning about HIV and Aids in our classrooms. Teachers themselves are generally misinformed as to the nature of HIV and Aids and its statistical insignificance when considering life-threatening causations.

Table 6 shows that in England and Wales cancer, pneumonia,

Table 6 **Death by selected causes (England & Wales) 1999**

All causes		556,118
Malignant neoplasms:		134,135
Digestive organs and peritoneum	37,333	
Trachea, bronchus, lung & pleura	29,968	
Breast (female)	11,604	
Ischaemic heart disease		115,119
Pneumonia		59,273
Cerebrovascular disease		56,051
Diabetes		5,963
Suicide		3,690
Motor vehicle accidents		2,942
All other accidents	7,702	
Accidental falls of which:		3,993
Fall on or from stairs in home	549	
Fall from chair or bed	97	
Slipping, tripping or stumbling	86	
Fall into hole in ground	5	
Accidental poisoning of which:		1,030
By medical drugs, medicaments, biologicals	812	
By alcohol	145	
By utility gas	50	
Aids		305
Choking on food		228
Accidental drowning		228
Suffocation by plastic bag		63
Choking on objects other than food		55
Struck accidentally by falling object		42
In the bathtub		33
Clothes catching fire		31
Meningococcal meningitis		27
Salmonella gastroenteritis		16
Injury caused by animals		13
In sports		10
Lightning		6
Hornets, wasps and bees		3
Dog bite		2
E. coli		2

Source: Mortality Statistics: National Statistics, cause DH2, 26

heart disease, suicide, accidents, poisoning and diabetes are all more likely to cause death than Aids.

The PHLS (Public Health Laboratory Service) published in 1999 cumulative figures (beginning when HIV seropositive was first reportable) for children between the ages of 0 and 14 years and 15 and 24 years registered as being seropositive. The figures reveal that in the whole of England 685 children between the ages of 0 and 14 years tested HIV seropositive. Remember, this is a cumulative total, spanning 20 years or so. Of these 685, 461 are in London. Most of these children will have parents who are drug users or have come to Britain from other countries; most will be non-white. In the 15–24 category, the total number testing HIV seropositive is 663, with 359 being in the capital. Figures are also given by region and by gender category. In the Northern and Yorkshire region, 33 young people in the 15–24 age group tested HIV seropositive. This figure is made up of 26 males and 7 females. In the North-west the total figure in this age group is 60 (53 males and 7 females). These figures indicate that girls are very unlikely to become HIV seropositive; those at risk are either homosexuals or drug users.

The number of medical problems likely to be encountered throughout one's lifetime that cause not only death but discomfort and ill heath are numerable. Some are the result of behavioural activities, such as smoking, excessive drinking or diet. Children can obviously be warned about the risks that they face if they partake in certain activities or conduct. Other factors that contribute to health problems and possibly death are exogenous to the individual's behaviour; that is, the disease cannot be prevented by the actions of the individual. These diseases, however, will generally have associated warning signs. If these are recognised at an early stage and treated promptly, death or further illness may be avoided.

Question: Is HIV and Aids education compulsory because it poses a significant threat to the health of the general population?
Answer: No. HIV and Aids do not, and never have, posed a significant health risk to the general population.

Conclusion

Drawing on our research in schools, we suggested that what was being taught under the banner of HIV and Aids, in compulsory lessons in England and Wales, seemed to be informed by five propositions. Having gone through the best available and latest scientific evidence, we are in a position to challenge each of these five propositions. Indeed, it would seem that the evidence supports, instead, the five propositions in Figure 2, which are the *opposite* to what is likely to be being taught in schools.

First, it is patently clear that all are *not* at the same risk of HIV seropositivity. Certain groups which engage in high-risk activities are very much at risk; for other members of the population the risk is negligible. Second, it is not true that all those with HIV antibodies progress on to Aids – it would seem that the majority do not. Third, a far better indicator of who progresses from HIV seropositivity to Aids is to identify who engages in high-risk behaviour. Fourth, HIV seropositivity is very much unlike other sexually transmitted infections in many ways, and should not be taught in schools as if it were identical. Finally, the risk of dying from Aids is tiny compared to other health risks, raising the question of why such a small risk merits compulsory inclusion in the school curriculum.

Figure 2 **Five alternative propositions on Aids and HIV**

---

(1) All are *not* at the same risk of becoming HIV seropositive; heterosexuals and homosexuals face very different risks. The same applies to drug users and non-drug users;

(2) Those with HIV seropositivity do *not* always proceed to develop Aids;

(3) HIV seropositivity does *not* progress to Aids at the same rate for all risk groups – in particular, heterosexual non-drug users from the UK do *not* have the same chance of becoming HIV seropositive and of progressing to Aids as any other risk group;

(4) HIV seropositivity is in all relevant respects *not* the same as other sexually transmitted infections;

(5) HIV seropositivity and Aids are *not* significant health risks, more significant than other risks, such as cancer and heart disease; as such their place in the compulsory school curriculum is called into question.

It is clear that the compulsory inclusion of HIV and Aids education in schools is unwarranted, given its statistical insignificance as a syndrome affecting the general public. Most of the population do not partake in the risk activities that are associated with HIV transmission. The clear conclusion from this chapter is that children are being misinformed about HIV and Aids, through a mis-education that is unnecessarily alarmist and not factually based.

4 BUT WHAT ABOUT AFRICA?

The problem of Africa

Everything that has been written thus far is open to the objection: but what about Africa? For it is well known, a part of the accepted wisdom, that Africa is in the midst of an Aids pandemic, and 'there but for the Grace of God' go we. Indeed, if funding levels and intensive sex education are not maintained, it is frequently asserted, then the same level of Aids disaster awaits us here. Only through continued vigilance can we stop descending into the same mire.

Does the evidence support this challenge to our position?

The arguments concern *sub-Saharan* Africa. The World Health Organisation (WHO) estimated that there were 34.3 million cases of HIV/Aids, of which 80 per cent were in sub-Saharan Africa, according to the Aids epidemic update by UNAids in June 2000. Although these figures are, on the face of it, startling, there emerge at least four anomalies which call into question some of the claims made about Aids and HIV in Africa, and their relevance to the situation in the UK.

Four anomalies

1 Why is Aids in Africa associated with common diseases, whereas Aids in the West is associated with rare ones?

Aids in Africa is certainly very different from Aids here. The main Aids-defining disease in Africa is tuberculosis (UNAids, 2000). In industrialised countries the main disease afflicting drug users is an unusual form of pneumonia (*Pneumocystis carinii)* and, in some homosexual men, Kaposi's sarcoma (a form of skin cancer). Why is this? The usual explanation is that those people with compromised immune systems succumb to the common infections. Thus those who are reported to have Aids in Africa die generally of tuberculosis, which is a common cause of death in that continent. However, the cause of death from a common infection becomes more problematic in explaining Aids in the West because pneumocystis and Kaposi's sarcoma are *not* common infections and were extremely rare prior to Aids. Thus there is a major difference between Aids in Africa and Aids in the West. In Africa, the main Aids-defining disease, tuberculosis, is endemic and a major cause of mortality. In some industrialised countries, there is a growing overlap between Aids and tuberculosis, especially among black Hispanic minorities living in deprived conditions in the USA. Expansions in criteria for Aids diagnosis have led to the inclusion of other common conditions, such as cancer of the uterine cervix, as Aids-defining diseases, so, artificially, the gap is closing. Even so, the majority of cases of Aids in industrial countries are succumbing to a pattern of disease which is, in severity and dimension, quite different from that in Africa.

2 Different diagnostic standards for HIV seropositivity in Africa

Disturbingly, the diagnosis of Aids in developing countries *does not require the same diagnostic standards as used in the developed countries, and often does not require a test for HIV*. Table 7 illustrates this anomaly. Tests that are compulsory for diagnosis of HIV seropositivity in Australia, the USA and the UK are *optional* in the confirmation of diagnosis in Africa.[1] Non-specialists need not be too concerned about the details in the table. The main reason for its inclusion is to draw out the major anomalies. For instance, in Africa it is optional whether or not proteins in the 'POL' and 'GAG' categories are found; in Australia and the USA, these are compulsory. The dimension of error in management and estimates due to this anomaly is unmeasured but obviously enormous since, in the worst-affected areas, facilities for laboratory-based diagnosis are lacking.

The results are often regarded as representative of the population and then projected to give estimates for the region or country as a whole. Confirmation by culture of the live virus is difficult and rarely performed.

---

1   For confirmation of HIV seropositivity, there are four ways of testing for HIV: the ELISA test, the Western Blot test, the polymerase chain reaction (PCR) test for viral DNA, and by viral culture itself. The ELISA test, which is the most commonly performed HIV test everywhere, gives a variable proportion of false positive results which overlap with other diseases endemic in Africa (Biggar, Gigase, Melbye et al., 1985). The concurrence of an ELISA positive with a Western Blot or PCR positive is assumed to confirm undated exposure to HIV. But these tests do not differentiate between infectious and non-infectious HIV (Stewart, 1994). Infectious means that the virus is having an adverse effect on the host. Non-infectious implies the virus is 'dormant' and causing no distress to the host's immune system. Any organism capable of causing infection when transferred from person to person is by definition infectious, but many can remain latent, that is, asymptomatic, for years, as in the case of shingles, tuberculosis and leprosy. In the best studies of Aids in Africa, HIV prevalence is identified by Western Blot or PCR as well as ELISA.

Table 7 Methods of testing for HIV seropositivity

Western Blot[1] 'viral proteins'	Africa	Australia	USA Food & Drug Admin.	USA Red Cross	USA CDC(2)[2]	USA CDC(3)[2]	USA CON[3]	USA MCACS[4]	UK[5]
ENV gene p160 p120 p41	any 2	1 or more	1 or more	1 or more	p120/p160 and p41	p120/p160 or p41	p120/p160 or p41	any 1 strong or 3 weak bands from: p15, p24, p32, p41, p45, p53, p55, p64, & p120.	1 or more
POL gene p68 p53 p32	optional any 3	any 3	p32	any 1	—	—	p32 or p24	Score '1' for each weak band, and '3' for each strong band – total of '3' or greater is positive.	p32
GAG gene p55 p40 p24 p18			p24	any 1	—	p24			p24

Source: Adapted from Turner, 1997

1 The Western Blot test for HIV seropositivity attempts to identify some of the proteins deemed to be part of the HIV. The table shows that the qualifying proteins differ within and across countries.

2 Center for Disease Control.

3 Consortium for Retrovirus Serology Standardisation.

4 Multi Center Aids Cohort Study (USA).

5 This test has been abandoned in the UK because of non-specific reaction but is still recommended for use in Africa where non-specific reactions are more common.

3 Assumption of HIV seropositivity and Aids without testing

Lack of facilities, as described above, leads also to inaccuracies in regions where other Aids-defining diseases such as tuberculosis, malaria, enteritis, malnutrition and leprosy are present. Individuals, groups of individuals or even whole regions are often presumed to be infected with HIV with or without a formal HIV seropositivity test. This is justified under clinical impression in the permissive classification agreed by the WHO and the US CDC (Centre for Disease Control) at Bangui in central Africa in 1985. By this classification, if an African suffers from any of the three following conditions, Aids can be officially diagnosed and registered.

- fever
- chronic or recurrent diarrhoea
- weight loss
- chronic cough
- any form of tuberculosis

4 High-incidence and low-incidence Aids countries in Africa have the same mean fertility, birth rate and rate of infant mortality

This is perhaps the greatest anomaly of all, and leads to the quite alarming conclusion that well-established endemic diseases in Africa such as tuberculosis, enteritis, malaria, schistosomiasis and malnutrition have simply been renamed Aids in some countries, but not in others. How do we arrive at this position?

First, it is incorrect to assume, as seems to happen in a great deal of popular discussion, that Aids in Africa affects all African countries more or less equally. The WHO publishes figures of Aids incidence in African countries. These can be divided into a high-

Table 8 **Socio-economic characteristics of high and low Aids incidence in African countries: cumulative data from 1985 to 18 January 2001**

	Africa (n = 52)	High (H) incidence (n = 19)	Low (L) incidence (n = 33)	Mann-Whitney Test
Mean Aids/ 100,000 (Sentinel)	150	337	42	0.0000
Median Aids/ 100,000 (Sentinel)	72	341	29	
Mean population growth % p.a.	2.4	2.3	2.4	0.7405
Mean birth rate per 1,000	38	39	37	0.9092
Mean death rate per 1,000	14	16	13	0.0653
Mean maternal death rate per 1,000,000	837	780	871	0.5989
Mean infant mortality per 1,000 live births	84	87	82	0.8567
Mean mortality <5 years per 1,000	146	129	156	0.1710
Mean life expectancy, years[1]	52	48	54	0.0264
Mean fertility: children born/woman	5	5	5	0.9922
Mean GDP per capita US$	863	697	965	0.7643

Source: www.unaids/hivaidsinfo/statistics/june98/fact_sheets/africa.html (The figures are incomplete for some years – for example, for South Africa. They were compiled from the UNAids website, January 2001.)

1 This is the only statistically significant difference at the 95 per cent confidence level. It might mean mortality due to poverty or Aids or it might mean a recurrence of endemic diseases or both. Follow-up and close investigation are essential.

n = number of African countries.

Sentinel = best diagnostic practice.

incidence group and a low-incidence group. Contrary to popular belief, Uganda only qualified in 1995 as a high-incidence country. Other high-incidence countries such as the Congo, the Ivory Coast and Togo on the west coast, and Djibouti and Kenya on the east coast, are separated from each other and the main high-Aids-incidence cluster of Zambia, Namibia, Malawi, Zimbabwe and Botswana by hundreds or thousands of miles. The geographically small but high-Aids-incidence country of Swaziland is surrounded by relatively low-incidence South Africa[2] and Mozambique. A comparison of socio-economic statistics of high- and low-incidence countries is shown in Table 8. Life expectancy is lower in the high- than in the low-Aids-incidence countries, but this could be accounted for since life expectancy is highly correlated with GNP per head (see Table 9).

Second, as far as a consensus is possible it is that Aids began in

2   South Africa is often quoted as a high-incidence country, but incomplete WHO sentinel numbers of Aids cases suggest it to be low-incidence.

3   This, in itself, is problematic; why was it not first identified there? If we accept that it migrated to America as a consequence of heterosexual transmission in visitors to Africa it appears unusual in re-emerging in San Francisco and New York bathhouses in clusters of homosexual men who had no previous contact with Africa. Or had they? Many African-Americans travelled to Africa to find their roots and could have acquired HIV there, according to the consensus. But they travelled mainly to West African territories (Senegal to the Niger), the areas in which slaves were bought or captured, where Aids is not nearly so common as it is in East Africa, which in turn is not readily accessible from the west coast. Alternatively, they could have taken Aids with them, for the first cases were not reported there until 1985, five years after the first cases were identified in California and New York City. Those cases were recognised farther south in Zaïre, and it has been suggested by an investigating journalist, Edward Hooper, in *The River*, that Aids began there as a consequence of alleged contamination of Poliomyelitis vaccine with SV40 or another similar virus which began to be used in the 1960s. Hooper's work was examined in detail at a recent meeting of the Royal Society, a surprising concession as the proposal is conjectural, journalistic and lacking in scientific evidence.

Table 9 **Socio-economic indicators of selected countries**

	Pop. (millions)	Rate of increase %	Maternal mortality per 100,000 live births	Infant mortality per 100,000 live births	Life exp. (years, male)	Fertility (children per woman)	GNP per capita US$
Botswana	1.3	2.4	250	58	46	4.4	3,209
Congo	1.8	3.0	890	90	46	6.1	702
Djibouti	0.08	2.9	570	106	49	5.3	979
Kenya	21.4	n/a[1]	650	66	51	4.5	356
Uganda	16.7	2.9	1,200	107	39	7.1	313
France	56.6	0.5	15	6	74	1.7	23,843
Italy	59.1	0.0	12	7	75	1.2	19,962
Spain	39.4	0.1	7	7	75	1.2	13,412
Switzerland	6.9	0.8	6	6	75	1.5	35,170
UK	56.3	0.2	9	7	75	1.7	21,921
USA	248.7	1.0	12	7	73	2.0	28,789

Source: United Nations Statistical Yearbook (2000), 44th edn 1997, data available as of 30 November 1999

1 Rate not available because of apparent lack of comparability between estimates shown for 1990 and 1997.

Africa. If that is the case,[3] it must have started years before it was first detected in the USA in 1981. If 1969 is accepted as the latest date, this would allow HIV to have been brought back immediately to New York and San Francisco and somehow to have infected homosexuals in these cities for a conservative incubation period of, say, ten years. It is therefore reasonable to expect, after thirty years, that some discernible effects will be apparent in Africa from national statistics of fertility, death rates and other indicators. Some commentators have stated that estimates of life expectancy in high-incidence countries will be reduced by six years by 2010 (Commission of the European Communities, 1993). The population growth of Kenya was expected to be halved by 2000.

However, the comparable figures on birth rates, death rates and fertility for Africa from the UN (Table 8) appear to contradict this. Given that HIV serves as a marker in Africa for sexually transmissible diseases of all types, and that fertility is diminished by such infections, the mean fertility and birth rates are startling. So too is the low rate of infant mortality, given the compromised immunological state of children born to women with HIV antibodies.

How can these figures be explained? All the differences in the chart except life expectancy can be explained by statistical chance. But this means that the averages of the high- and low-incidence countries are, for interpretative purposes, equal; there is no difference in these characteristics between high- and low-incidence countries. This leads to the possibility that well-established endemic diseases such as tuberculosis have been renamed Aids in some countries (the high-incidence ones) but not in others (the low-incidence ones).

Reinterpreting Aids in Africa

The figures in Table 9 indicate how poor African countries are. With poverty on the African scale malnutrition, an unambiguous cause of compromised immunity, is widespread. In tropical Africa, Aids and HIV seropositivity are virtually synonymous with regions where malaria is endemic (Root-Bernstein, 1993: 304) with a high mortality in the younger age groups. From data collected for the WHO from 1970 to 1975 it was concluded that in Kenya (high-incidence) and Nigeria (low-incidence), malaria was responsible for about 25 per cent of infant mortality. Those surviving malaria often develop anaemia, which is frequently treated by blood transfusions, which may or may not be screened for HIV antibodies and other viral and bacterial contaminants. In low-in-cidence Democratic Republic of the Congo (formerly Zaïre), be-tween 1985 and 1986 70 per cent of 13,000 transfusions were given to children with malaria. There is a medical consensus that blood transfusions in themselves stress and may deplete the body's im-mune defences. In some African medical practices unsterilised needles and shared syringes are used on a scale that would be in-tolerable in industrialised countries. Pathogenic and other conta-minants are thereby transmitted in blood transfusions and inoculations with penicillin and other injected drugs and vaccines. To this can be added the officially unacknowledged but widely known drug abuse problem in many African countries. African people have, for decades, experienced rampant tuberculosis, lym-phomas, chronic diarrhoea and other diseases registrable as Aids under the International Classification of Diseases (1993) which have caused millions of deaths. There is also a huge incidence of all forms of sexually transmitted diseases. All of this, combined with inadequate medical care, contamination and shortage of water and food, huge population movements and the diseases which ac-company political revolution and war, contributes strongly to the increase of Aids-defining diseases in Africa.

The absence of difference in population statistics between African countries with high and low incidence of Aids means that reports of a destructive pandemic of catastrophic dimensions are at present unfounded. The mix of Aids-defining diseases in Africa, which were also common before Aids, is certainly completely dif-ferent from that in the industrialised countries. This should not be interpreted only as implying that Aids in Africa is a redefining of old-established endemic diseases as Aids – though it is *precisely* this which has been reported as the African Aids tragedy. However, it is clear from medical reports that some of the Aids diseases of the industrialised countries are also present in the big African cities. Whether these Aids diseases in African cities can also be explained as the consequences of high-risk behaviour such as drug abuse or anal sex seems unlikely, but this is an important issue which demands investigation. It is imperative that the assumed differences between industrial countries' and African Aids receive critical investigation to support a new syndrome of Aids in Africa, where there is one, distinct from a background incidence of endemic diseases. Given the massive funding accorded on the basis of estimates of Aids taken at face value, there is the possibility that other, more prevalent and equally dangerous diseases are being denied attention and funding.

In short, the situation in Africa is sufficiently ambiguous to prevent us from arriving at any clear-cut challenge to the position reached at the end of Chapter 3. There is an immense problem which clearly demands open-minded and searching investigation of contributory causes but, at the present time, there is no evidence to suggest that the much-reported Aids pandemic in Africa is what is in store for us here.

5 EXPLAINING PUBLIC POLICY ON AIDS AND HIV

Three explanations for public policy

The decline in the number of Aids cases has been attributed to the decisions taken at the end of the 1980s to provide grotesquely generous funds for prevention initiatives (Craven, Stewart & Taghavi, 1994, 1996). These public monies fund the only medical syndrome with more attendant workers than patients (Craven & Stewart, 1995). It is also claimed that the funds allocated to Aids and HIV prevention have prevented incidence of the syndrome and of HIV seropositivity in France, Spain and Italy. The same explanation is given for the failure of HIV to move into the general heterosexual population. Even greater claims for the efficacy of the funding have been made since the early and mid 1990s. Now it is asserted that, without the generous and imaginative funding of sex education, the UK would be experiencing an epidemic of sub-Saharan proportions. The argument of the previous chapters is that none of these claims is sustainable. The passage of time and the explosive increase of all other forms of STIs since then make these claims untenable.

How, then, can we explain public policy on Aids and HIV, public policy that has found its way into the educational arena through a compulsory, although content-less, curriculum?

Here are three, not necessarily mutually incompatible explanations for the present public policy towards combating the problem of Aids. It may be that there are additional explanations, but the history of Aids suggests that these are the most likely.

A correct theory of causation?

The first explanation is that public policy is based upon a correct theory of causation. The medical consensus is that all those testing HIV seropositive will develop Aids, which is incurable and eventually fatal – the Virus-Aids hypothesis.

Is this a correct theory? The discussion thus far suggests not. A simple reason why present public policy, which is based on the assumption that all HIV seropositives will develop Aids, should be questioned is that the expert epidemiological predictions of the number of Aids cases have been consistently exaggerated. An official committee chaired by Sir David Cox, President of the Royal Statistical Society, reviewed available data and predicted (Department of Health and the Welsh Office) in 1988 that there would be at best about 2,400 new cases and at worst 15,440 new cases in Britain in 1992, giving cumulative totals of 9,330 to 34,077 in 1992. For planning, they suggested a figure of 3,600 new cases in Britain and a cumulative total of 12,750. Table 1 shows that the actual number of new cases diagnosed in 1992 was 1,578 and the cumulative total was 7,762. A symposium of experts convened by the Royal Society in the following year provided sophisticated mathematical models which confirmed these estimates (Cox, Anderson and Hillier, 1989), although revised methods from surveillance data in the Public Health Laboratory Service reports gave lower projections. A more accurate estimate was obtained in that year by a regression method based on the assumption that

Aids was increasing in the original risk groups, and that spreading by heterosexual transmission in the general population was minimal (Stewart, 1992a, b). Application of this method to New York City, with a much higher annual incidence, correctly predicted about 45,000 cases by the end of 1992. The actual total was 44,231. These errors in official projections have never been acknowledged or admitted and – what is more serious – the assumptions, concepts and methods are still being used for estimates internationally.

All this suggests that the first explanation is untenable.

A politically convenient hypothesis?

The second explanation is that the Virus-Aids hypothesis is politically convenient for the electorate.

Day and Klein (1989) discussed, in the context of Aids, how government policies may be formulated in response to an event which is new, unpredictable, unprojectable and problematic because of moral ambiguities. When Aids emerged it was a new syndrome. Aids involved sex, and this differentiated it from other problems of social policy such as unemployment, smoking or an influenza epidemic. The fear and panic which followed the pessimistic pronouncements of the medical profession, politicians and other groups after 1984, when it was postulated that the syndrome would move rapidly through the heterosexual community, created an environment in which resource decisions had to be made quickly. It would not be surprising if crisis management explained some of the disparate funding (Weeks, 1989).

The government, with no information of its own, was in a position rather like that of a naive patient when confronted with the news that he has a usually terminal cancer. As occurred subsequently with vCJD, assumed to be linked to BSE, the government turned for information to 'experts', and was subsequently presented with figures produced by an array of epidemiologists, actuaries, biostatisticians and statisticians with wide confidence intervals of long-term projections of the numbers of Aids cases.

The medical establishment was united, however, in believing that the cause of Aids was HIV. This medical consensus was convenient for politicians (Rose, 1987), avoiding expert dispute about a politically and morally sensitive issue. Moreover, the consensus proposed an explanation easy to understand: HIV = Aids = death. By comparison, the alternative hypothesis, that susceptibility to Aids was determined primarily by risk behaviour (Stewart, 1992a), was more subtle and complex, and suggested that Aids was caused by changes in sexual behaviour – an explanation that was at variance with the politically correct culture. The government knew but did not admit that there was a geographical concentration of cases in inner London and, to a lesser extent, in Edinburgh and Brighton. Aids was portrayed by the media as a potential threat to the provinces through the radiation of cases. It was seen as a threat to the country about which something had to be done, yet no one knew quite what.

In the event the government followed the precautionary principle (Craven & Stewart, 1997) – what Kent Weaver (1986) has called 'the politics of blame avoidance'. As subsequently with BSE, it had to be seen to be taking Aids seriously. It increased, by enormous amounts, the research budgets and funds for treatment and implemented a huge health education prevention programme in the media.

The response demonstrated further the principle that in

circumstances involving ethical and emotional issues, such as Northern Ireland and the monarchy, politicians are likely to make issues non-party-political and ignore voter preferences as signalled to them, relying instead on the advice of experts. By making the issue bipartisan the government removed the checks and balance in the form of doubts and questions from opposition parties which are generally raised in all other areas of policy-making. But if the political response of huge funding can be explained by its being electorally convenient, the justification for it cannot.

Rent-seeking by producer and interest groups?

A third possible explanation is that of 'rent-seeking' by producer and interest groups.

We have argued that current funding for Aids cannot be justified on the conventional medical grounds of containing an epidemic because there is not, and never has been, an epidemic of either Aids cases or of HIV in the UK. Perhaps the continuing extraordinarily generous expenditure on Aids can be explained as being in the interests of service-providers. Wherever there is an information vacuum, rent-seekers (rent is the name given by economists to returns on activities which generate incomes in excess of those which would be earned in competitive conditions) are advantaged; they have greater incentives to acquire funding and less need to substantiate their case. The Aids situation of the mid-1980s was almost certainly conducive to exploitation by producer and interest groups. Rose (1987) has stated that experts, because they are scientists, tend to give a high priority to their own expertise to the exclusion of competing specialists with competing interests. In the case of interest groups a noteworthy example is provided by Kaposi's sarcoma, a disease found disproportionately in homosexual Aids cases. It is still classified as an Aids disease even in the absence of HIV antibodies, and this is indicative of the influence of the gay rights interest groups. In this case seropositivity to HIV was waived at the discretion of those making the diagnosis.

Although homosexual groups in the United States had consistently campaigned for recognition that Aids was a general social threat, it was only the discovery of HIV seropositivity in female drug users and haemophiliacs which initiated current funding levels (Shilts, 1987). Elsewhere in medicine, interest groups include the specialists and researchers in genitourinary medicine, virologists and immunologists, all of whom have a professional interest in the Virus-Aids hypothesis. This, in turn, has led to rent-seeking by pharmaceutical companies from the sale of Elisa, Western Blot and PCR test kits for indirect identification of the virus. The pharmaceutical companies have, in addition, interests in developing patented drugs, such as protease inhibitors, to attempt to slow the progression of HIV, and also in financing research trials to confirm their efficacy. Following the news of the Concorde trial, which cast doubt on the efficacy of zidovudine (AZT) in slowing the progress towards Aids in asymptomatic HIV patients, the share price of Wellcome fell by 6 per cent in a week. In December 1993 American sales of AZT had fallen by 25 per cent by comparison with the same month the previous year.

The market has an even greater commercial incentive to develop and promote a vaccine to prevent Aids because this would be given to everyone deemed to be at risk, either by being seropositive or by being in a risk group or location. In some situations, the expanded classification would mean that almost everyone except those already moribund from Aids would be eligible to receive such a vaccine on one or more occasions. If it were shown to be effective – and this would not be difficult because most people, even if seropositive, do not or do not necessarily develop Aids – the market would conceivably be greater than that for any other drug or vaccine!

As the medical profession has accepted that HIV is the cause of Aids, so administrative structures have been financed which provide employment to hundreds of non-professional workers. The extent of this employment, directly by the health authorities and indirectly by organisations many of which are not subject to formal audit, is without medical precedent.

There is another important factor to support the view that Aids funding has been influenced by service-provider pressure. As the number of people testing HIV seropositive but without Aids increased, the medical profession thrice changed the definition. This is well documented. In 1987 the CDC redefined Aids to include several additional illnesses which increased immediately the number of Aids cases (Centers for Disease Control, 1987). In 1992/3 the CDC again redefined Aids to include invasive carcinoma of the cervix, tuberculosis and other prevalent conditions in serologically positive persons (International Classification of Diseases, 1993). The new definition is justified as a means of securing support under national programmes for the ethnic minorities in the United States who are majorities in the Third World. It immediately increased the incidence and cumulative prevalence since 1982 of Aids in the United States by more than 50 per cent, from 250,000 to over 400,000 cases. Aids ceased, overnight, to be a mainly male disease (Stewart, 1992c). In 1998, in the face of declining cases, the definition was changed again to include all persons who were seropositive to HIV, irrespective of absence of symptoms. These redefinitions, which were arranged *in camera* by the US CDC and the World Health Organisation, have led to enormous increases in cases in developing countries, where even the dubious sanction of seropositivity to HIV is no longer required.

These definitional changes have made Aids a heterosexual and more widely prevalent disease, enhancing the claims of all producer and interest groups associated with Aids.

In the politically sensitive public healthcare sector, government funding changes year on year are not volatile. Budget decision-making in the next period will largely be determined by what has happened in the present period. There have been incremental increases in NHS funding each year over the past decade. Wildavsky (1975) commented that 'once enacted a budget becomes a precedent: the fact that something has been done before vastly increases the chances that it will be done again'. And there are good reasons for this. Zero-based budgeting, where decision-makers start afresh in each time period, is not practical. Decision-makers face bounded rationality in a world of complexity (Williamson, 1973). It is not possible for them to take all eventualities into account. In the case of Aids, the policy-makers were constrained not only by their own limited knowledge of medical matters, but also by disagreement among their expert advisers and by the need to be seen as not discriminating against homosexuals. Having decided initially to allocate huge ring-fenced funds, unprecedented in magnitude and unquestioned by the opposition parties, conditions were ripe for interest groups to exploit and consolidate their position.

6 CONCLUSIONS AND A
WAY FORWARD

Education about HIV and Aids provides a revealing and perplexing case study of the workings of government in education. It carries lessons about the particulars of sex education and the role of schools in promoting or dissuading certain types of sexual behaviour, of course. But it also carries more general lessons for education policy at large, and the problems of government intervention in education.

When Aids was first recognised as a syndrome in the 1980s it was presented as a new health threat, it was always fatal, and there was no cure. Allegations of spread by heterosexual transmission of HIV appeared to put the general public at risk. The Conservative government, after intense lobbying by special interest groups and the BBC *Today* programme, felt the need to 'do something' about Aids and HIV. And one of the things that it did was to introduce in all schools in England and Wales the compulsory requirement that they provide teaching about HIV and Aids. We showed in Chapter 1 how the progress of the law provides a classic case of the unintended consequences of government intervention in a controversial cause. The executive wanted to do something, but countervailing forces, particularly in the House of Lords, reflected concerns that this would mean 'doing something' distasteful in schools. The result was the unhappy compromise that we now see: schools compelled to teach a topic about which no content can be provided by government. And if no content is being provided by government, this means in practice that schools become the target for a range of special interest groups. This is a recipe for propaganda and miseducation.

The rot started in 1991 when the National Curriculum for Science was amended for children aged eleven to fourteen to include study of HIV and Aids, both behavioural and biological. But some Conservative backbenchers and members of the House of Lords felt that such instruction would inevitably involve the teaching of homosexual practices. A pamphlet on HIV and Aids for schools produced by the then Department for Education confirmed these suspicions: it was judged as being 'amoral' and 'judgement free' in the House of Lords, and criticised for 'explicitly describing oral sex' and 'deviant sexual practices'. Thus the compromise of the 1993 Education Act. The science curriculum was amended to take out the study of HIV/Aids 'other than biological aspects'; at the same time, sex education would have to be a compulsory part of the 'basic curriculum' to be provided by all maintained secondary schools. And sex education – the first time it had ever been defined by law – must now include education about the behavioural aspects of HIV and Aids. Guidance would be provided, but, to satisfy the disgruntled Lords, no explicit material, not even the tiniest bit of content. It is the responsibility of each individual school to gather the information that it is to deliver in its programme.

To find out what this means in practice, we visited local schools and LEA officials, to see how they were finding material to use, and what lessons they were conveying in schools. From our visits, described in Chapter 2, we gained the impression of special interest groups foisting on schools material that teachers seemed not adequately equipped to judge. And, partly because of these materials, all the lessons we saw 'normalised' HIV and Aids. We found five clear messages coming through, including that *all* are at the same risk of becoming HIV seropositive – heterosexual and homosexual, drug users and non-drug users. And that all testing HIV seropositive proceed to develop Aids, and HIV seropositivity progresses to Aids at the same rate for all risk groups, so it does not matter what your behaviour is – once diagnosed HIV seropositive, you will inevitably proceed to Aids.

But once the scientific evidence is examined, as it was in Chapter 3, it becomes increasingly hard to see how these assumptions can be supported. For instance, from the date that Aids was first diagnosed to 2000 there have been over 43,000 people diagnosed HIV seropositive in the UK. Less than 1 per cent are thought to have become infected through heterosexual intercourse where there is no evidence of a high-risk partner or of infection outside Europe. These facts, and any implications that might arise from them, are singularly avoided in HIV/Aids lessons. Teachers are at pains, mainly because the material they use is one-sided, to stress that all are equally at risk. And this is the message that we heard coming through loud and clear from students of all ages: 'You can get Aids equally well from sex with men or women, or from taking drugs. Even your mum can give it to you.' The special interest groups have reason to be well pleased.

It might be argued that the figures showing a reduction in the incidence of Aids reveal that HIV and Aids education is clearly having a positive impact, leading to young people changing their sexual behaviour, in particular not having unprotected sexual intercourse. Unfortunately, such optimism is belied by the number of teenage pregnancies and increasing rates of infections from other sexually transmitted diseases. The frequency of cases of sexually transmitted infections such as gonorrhoea and chlamydia rose rapidly between 1995 and 1999. Although conceptions to women in England generally fell by 6.1 per cent between 1991 and 1997, there has been a small increase in the number of conceptions by mothers under the age of sixteen. The attempt to normalise sex, provided that it is 'always with a condom', the constant theme in the HIV and Aids education materials, is apparently not having the desired effect.

But does not the situation in Africa show that there is a terrible danger in becoming complacent about HIV and Aids? We examined the evidence here in Chapter 4, and concluded that, at best, the evidence is inconclusive. There were at least four anomalies noted. First, Aids in Africa is associated with common diseases, such as tuberculosis, whereas Aids in the West is associated with rare ones. Second, it appears that diagnosis of HIV in Africa does not require the same diagnostic standards as are used in the developed countries, so we cannot really be sure whether HIV as we know it here has actually been detected there. Third, some clinical units seem to find instances of an Aids-related disease, such as tuberculosis, malaria, malnutrition, etc., in Africa and simply assume the presence of HIV seropositivity without testing for it. Finally, the finding that high-incidence and low-incidence Aids countries in Africa have the same mean fertility, birth rates and rates of infant mortality is very odd indeed. It raises the possibility that many apparent cases of Aids in the high-incidence countries are simply due to a reclassification of existing diseases, or the consequence of a testing procedure which registers as having Aids all who are seropositive to HIV (Stewart, 2001).

Each of these considerations raises the issue of why HIV and Aids education should have such a privileged place in the school curriculum. To put it in perspective, in 1999 305 people died from Aids in the UK. More people died from falling down stairs (549) and almost as many died from choking on food (228). Yet we never hear calls to celebrate World Choking Day in schools, nor demands for 'advice on avoiding death from falling down stairs' to become a compulsory part of the curriculum. And the figures are positively dwarfed by problems from other diseases. About 60,000 people die each year from pneumonia and 250,000 from cancer and heart disease. Clearly something else is at work here, apart from actual risk of ill health. In Chapter 5 we outlined a couple of hypotheses that could explain public policy on HIV and Aids – including education policy – and found the explanation of 'rent-seeking' by producer and interest groups particularly persuasive.

But with so many powerful vested interest groups – including pharmaceutical companies and health professionals – with so much to gain from existing policy and so much to lose from any change, the difficulties of bringing about any reform are compounded. Does this mean that reform is impossible? We are concerned in this paper fundamentally with education policy. Can anything be done to avoid the types of situation documented in Chapter 2 from continuing in schools?

One solution which may have occurred to some readers, of course, would be not only to compel schools to provide teaching about HIV and Aids, but to make the *content* compulsory too. And 'right-minded' thinkers could then lobby government, and influence political parties and their agendas, to ensure that the kinds of ideas presented in this book, in Chapters 3 and 4 in particular, are the ones that find their way into schools, not those that are currently there.

To draw this conclusion would be a terrible mistake, for two reasons. The first is that the issues are far too controversial. And controversial issues make for bad state compulsion. Even if one party could agree that a particular content was preferable, and even if that party were elected, it would still have to get its policy through the various tiers of government, and at each level the vested interest groups would lobby. At each step of the way there would be the danger that content would get distorted and that opposing views would creep in. And, most seriously of all, if one party created the precedent that the content of this controversial area of sex education could be prescribed, then there would be absolutely no protection from another opposing view winning influence and prescribing an altogether more destructive curriculum on unsuspecting schools.

The second reason is much more fundamental. The main thesis of this paper is that there is something very odd, indeed very unwholesome, about making HIV and Aids compulsory subjects in the school curriculum at all. Their inclusion seems more to do with prurient fascination rather than any significant health risk to the population. In short, they have no place in the curriculum.

Rather than seeking to impose a particular content, government should be persuaded to withdraw from this area altogether. What is needed is to repeal the law which states that HIV and Aids teaching must be compulsory in schools. Part of the challenge is recognising the legal oddity of having a compulsory controversial topic without compulsory content. But this must be coupled with an acknowledgement of the dangers of trying to make compulsory any particular curriculum, given the controversy underlying the issues. Above all, it must be combined with recognition of the fact that government intervention in a topic that poses no threat at all to the majority of the population is unnecessary.

What would happen if some schools quietly decided to jettison this aspect of the school curriculum? Would there be any come-back? Perhaps this should be the preferred policy approach. Those who find the curriculum distasteful in this area should seek to have it removed from their schools, and allow politicians to catch up with this minor act of civil disobedience. Perhaps school governors and parents reading this book, realising what is happening in their schools, and realising its lack of scientific basis, should quietly ask their schools to drop this part of the compulsory curriculum. Certainly the four authors of this paper would be among those offering their support to any school that wanted to move forward in this way.

REFERENCES

Allen, I. (1987), 'Education in Sex and Personal Relationships',
Policy Studies Institute.

Anderson, R. M., Cox, D., Hillier, B. M. (1989), 'Symposium on
Epidemiological and Statistical Aspects of Aids', *Phil. Trans.
B.*, Royal Society, London.

Bainham, A. (1993), *Children: the Modern Law*, Jordan.

Barre-Sinoussi, F. et al. (1983), 'Isolation of a T-Lymphotropic
Retrovirus from a Patient at Risk from Acquired Immune
Deficiency Syndrome (Aids)', *Science*, 220: 868–71.

Biggar, R. J., Gigase, P. L., Melbye M. et al. (1985), 'ELISA HTLV
retrovirus antibody reactivity associated with malaria and
immune complexes in healthy Africans', *Lancet*, 2: 520–3.

Bridgeman, J. (1996), 'Don't tell the children: The Department's
guidance on the provision of information about
contraception to individual pupils', in Harris (1996b).

Centers for Disease Control (1987), 'Revision of the CDC
Surveillance Case Definition for Aids', *Morbidity and Mortality
Weekly Review*, 36: 35–155.

Centers for Disease Control (1992), '1993 Revised Classification
System for HIV Infection and Expanded Surveillance Case
Definition for Aids among Adolescents and Adults', *Morbidity
and Mortality Weekly Report*, 41: 1–19; with addendum to the
Proposed Expansion of the Aids Surveillance Case Definition,
October, Atlanta, Georgia.

Commission of the European Communities (1993), 'Draft paper on EC Aids policy in developing countries', 7 September: 13.

Courouce, A., Muller, A., and Richard, B. (1986), 'False positive Western Blot Reactions to HIV-1 in Blood Donors', *Lancet*, 2: 921–2.

Cox, D. R., Anderson, R. M., and Hillier, H. C. (eds) (1989), 'Epidemiological and Statistical Aspects of the Aids Epidemic', *Phil Trans S Soc*, London (B), 325, 37: 187.

Craven, B. M., and Stewart, G. T. (1995), 'Corporate Governance, Financial Reporting, Regulation and the Aids Threat in Scotland', *Financial Accountability and Management*, 11, 3: 223–40.

Craven, B. M., and Stewart, G. T. (1997), 'Public Policy and Public Health; coping with potential medical disaster', in Bate, R., *What Risked*, Butterworth-Heinemann, Oxford.

Craven, B. M., Stewart, G. T., and Taghavi, M. (1994), 'Amateurs Confronting Politicians: A Case Study of Aids in England', *Journal of Public Policy*, 13, 4: 305–25.

Craven, B. M., Stewart, G. T., and Taghavi, M. (1996), 'Aids: Regulation and Accountability of Expenditure in England in Relation to Epidemiological Determinants', in *Management Accounting in Health Care*, CIMA.

Davy, R. T., Dayton, L. R., Metcalf, J. A. et al. (1992), 'Intermediate WB patterns in a Cohort at High Risk for HIV Infection', *Journal of Clinical Immunology*, 12, 3: 185–92.

Day, P., and Klein, R. (1989), 'Interpreting the Unexpected: the case of Aids policymaking in Britain', *Journal of Public Policy*, 9, 3: 337–53.

Department for Education (1994), 'Education Act 1993: Sex Education in Schools' (Circular 5/94).

Department of Education and Employment (2000), 'Sex and Relationship Education Guidance', DfEE, London.

Department of Health (1999), 'Unlinked anonymous HIV surveys steering groups: Prevalence of HIV in the UK'. Data to end 1998. PHLS, London.

Department of Health and the Welsh Office (1988), 'Short Term Prediction of HIV Infection and Aids. Report of a working group' (Chairman Sir D. Cox), HMSO, London.

Duesberg, P. H. (1991), *Is the HIV Aids theory all wrong?*, CalReport.

Duesberg, P. H. (1996), *Inventing the Aids Virus*, Regnery Press.

Education (No. 2) Act 1986, HMSO.

Education Reform Act 1988 (Chapter 40), HMSO.

Education Act 1993 (Chapter 35), HMSO.

Education Act 1996 (Chapter 56), HMSO.

European Study Group on heterosexual transmission of HIV (1992), 'HIV transmission from men to women', *British Medical Journal*, 304: 811.

Gottlieb, M. S. (1981), 'Pneumocystis Carinii and Mucosal Candidiasis in Previously Healthy Homosexual Men', *New England Journal of Medicine*, 305, 24.

Harries, A. D. (1990), 'Tuberculosis and human immunodeficiency virus infection in developing countries', *Lancet*, 335: 387–90.

Harris, N. (1993), *Law and Education: Regulation, Consumerism and the Education System*, Sweet and Maxwell.

Harris, N. (1996a), 'The Regulation and Control of Sex Education', in Harris (1996b).

Harris, N. (ed.) (1996b), *Children, Sex Education and the Law*, Sex Education Forum, National Children's Bureau.

Harrison, J. K. (2000), *Sex Education in Secondary Schools*, Open
University Press.

Hearst, N., and Hulley, S. B. (1988), 'Preventing the Heterosexual
Spread of A.I.D.S.', *Journal of the American Medical
Association*, 259, 16: 2,429.

Hill, Graham (1993), *Science Single and Double Awards GCSE
National Curriculum Key Stage 4*, Letts Study Guide, BPP Letts
Education, London.

Hirschmann, A. O. (1970*), Exit, Voice and Loyalty: Responses to
Decline in Firms, Organisations, and States*, Harvard University
Press, Cambridge, MA.

International Classification of Diseases (1993), 10th ed., WHO,
Geneva.

Kent Weaver, R. (1986), 'The Politics of Blame Avoidance',
Journal of Public Policy, 6, 4: 371–98.

Learning and Skills Act 2000 (Chapter 21), HMSO.

Lees, J., and Plant, S. (2000), *PASSPORT: A framework for personal
and social development*, Calouste Gulbenkian Foundation,
London.

Lundberg, G. D. (1988), 'Serological Diagnosis of HIV Infection
by Western Blot Testing', *Journal of the American Medical
Association*, 260: 674–9.

Meyer, K. B., and Panker, S. G. (1987), 'Screening for HIV; Can
We Afford the False Positive Rate?', *New England Journal of
Medicine*, 317: 238–41.

Midthun, K., Garrison, G., Clements, M. L. et al. (1990),
'Frequency of Indeterminant Western Blot Tests in Healthy
Adults at Low Risk for HIV Infection', *Journal of Infectious
Diseases*, 162: 1379–82.

Monk, D. (1998), 'Sex Education and HIV/Aids: Political Conflict and Legal Resolution', *Children and Society*, 12: 295–305.

Mortimer, P. P. (1991), 'The Fallibility of HIV Western Blot', *Lancet*, 37: 286–7.

Padian, N. S., Shiboski, S. C., and Jewell, N. P. (1990), 'The effect of number of exposures on the risk of heterosexual HIV transmission', *Journal of Infectious Diseases*, 16: 883–7.

Parliament (House of Lords) (2000), Learning and Skills Bill.

Public Health Laboratory Service, 'Aids/HIV Quarterly Surveillance Tables Nos 1–50', unpublished, www.phls.co.uk/facts/HIV/hivqnotes.htm.

Quinn, T. C. (1996), 'Global Burden of the HIV Pandemic', *Lancet*, 348: 99–106.

Root-Bernstein, R. S. (1993), *Rethinking Aids*, Free Press, New York.

Root-Bernstein, R. S. (1995), 'Five myths about Aids that have misdirected research and treatment', *Genetica*, 95: 111–32.

Rose, R. (1987), 'The Political Appraisal of Employment Policies', *Journal of Public Policy*, 7, 3: 285–305.

Rowley, C. K. (1969), 'The Political Economy of British Education', *Scottish Journal of Political Economy*, 16: 152–76.

Scottish Home and Health Department (1996), 'Aids in Scotland: Predictions to the end of 1993 and 1996'. See also Scottish Centre for Infection and Environmental Health (SCIEH), Weekly Reports, 1993–9.

Shilts, R. (1987), *And the Band Played On: Politics, People and the Aids Epidemic*, Penguin Books, Harmondsworth.

Stewart, G. T. (1989), 'Uncertainties about HIV and Aids', *Lancet*, 1: 1325.

Stewart, G. T. (1992a), 'Epidemiology and Transmission of Aids', *The Society of Public Health Official Handbook and Members*

List: 19–24.

Stewart, G. T. (1992b), 'Errors in predictions of the incidence and distribution of Aids', *Lancet*, 341: 898.

Stewart, G. T. (1992c), 'Changing Case Definition for Aids', *Lancet*, 340: 1414.

Stewart, G. T. (1993), 'Aids Predictions', *Lancet*, 341: 1287.

Stewart, G. T. (1994), 'Scientific Surveillance and the Control of Aids: a call for open debate', *Health Care Analysis*, 2: 279–86.

Stewart, G. T. (1995), 'The Epidemiology and Transmission of Aids: a hypothesis linking behavioural and biological determinants with time, person and place', *Genetica*, 95: 173–85.

Stewart, G. T. (2001), 'HIV/Aids in Africa', *Aids and Hepatitis Digest*, Royal Society of Medicine Press, 83: 2–4.

Thatcher, M. (1993), *The Downing Street Years*, HarperCollins, London.

Tooley, J. (1995), *Disestablishing the School*, Avebury, Aldershot.

Tooley, J. (2000), *Reclaiming Education*, Cassell/Continuum, London.

UNAids (2000) , 'Report on the global HIV/AIDS epidemic', www.UNAIDS.org/epidemic_update/report/Epi_report.pdf

Turner, Dr Valendar F. (1997), 'Do antibody tests prove HIV infection?', interview, *Continuum*, 5, 2: 10–19.

Weeks, J. (1989), 'Aids: The Intellectual Agenda', in P. Aggleton, G. Hart and P. Davies (eds), *Aids: Social Representations, Social Practices*, Falmer Press: 1–21.

Wildavsky, A. (1975), *Budgeting: A Comparative Theory of Budgetary Processes*, Little, Brown and Co., Boston, MA.

Williamson, O. E. (1973), *Markets and Hierarchies: Analysis and Anti-Trust Implications*, Free Press, New York.

Zagury, D., Bernard, J., Leibowitch, J. et al. (1984), 'HTLV-III in cells cultured from semen of two patients with Aids', *Science*, 226: 449–51.

ABOUT THE IEA

The Institute is a research and educational charity (No. CC 235 351), limited by guarantee. Its mission is to improve understanding of the fundamental institutions of a free society with particular reference to the role of markets in solving economic and social problems.

The IEA achieves its mission by:

- a high-quality publishing programme
- conferences, seminars, lectures and other events
- outreach to school and college students
- brokering media introductions and appearances

The IEA, which was established in 1955 by the late Sir Antony Fisher, is an educational charity, not a political organisation. It is independent of any political party or group and does not carry on activities intended to affect support for any political party or candidate in any election or referendum, or at any other time. It is financed by sales of publications, conference fees and voluntary donations.

In addition to its main series of publications the IEA also publishes a quarterly journal, *Economic Affairs*, and has two specialist programmes – Environment and Technology, and Education.

The IEA is aided in its work by a distinguished international Academic Advisory Council and an eminent panel of Honorary Fellows. Together with other academics, they review prospective IEA publications, their comments being passed on anonymously to authors. All IEA papers are therefore subject to the same rigorous independent refereeing process as used by leading academic journals.

IEA publications enjoy widespread classroom use and course adoptions in schools and universities. They are also sold throughout the world and often translated/reprinted.

Since 1974 the IEA has helped to create a world-wide network of 100 similar institutions in over 70 countries. They are all independent but share the IEA's mission.

Views expressed in the IEA's publications are those of the authors, not those of the Institute (which has no corporate view), its Managing Trustees, Academic Advisory Council members or senior staff.

Members of the Institute's Academic Advisory Council, Honorary Fellows, Trustees and Staff are listed on the following page.

The Institute gratefully acknowledges financial support for its publications programme and other work from a generous benefaction by the late Alec and Beryl Warren.

99

For information about subscriptions to IEA publications, please contact:

Subscriptions
The Institute of Economic Affairs
2 Lord North Street
London SW1P 3LB

Tel: 020 7799 8900
Fax: 020 7799 2137
Website: www.iea.org.uk/books/subscribe.htm

Other papers recently published by the IEA include:

WHO, What and Why?

Transnational Government, Legitimacy and the World Health Organization
Roger Scruton
Occasional Paper 113
ISBN 0 255 36487 3

The World Turned Rightside Up

A New Trading Agenda for the Age of Globalisation
John C. Hulsman
Occasional Paper 114
ISBN 0 255 36495 4

The Representation of Business in English Literature

Introduced and edited by Arthur Pollard

Readings 53

ISBN 0 255 36491 1

Anti-Liberalism 2000

The Rise of New Millennium Collectivism

David Henderson

Occasional Paper 115

ISBN 0 255 36497 0

Capitalism, Morality and Markets

Brian Griffiths, Robert A. Sirico, Norman Barry & Frank Field

Readings 54

ISBN 0 255 36496 2

A Conversation with Harris and Seldon
Ralph Harris & Arthur Seldon
Occasional Paper 116
ISBN 0 255 36498 9

Malaria and the DDT Story
Richard Tren & Roger Bate
Occasional Paper 117
ISBN 0 255 36499 7

**A Plea to Economists Who Favour Liberty:
Assist the Everyman**
Daniel B. Klein
Occasional Paper 118
ISBN 0 255 36501 2

Waging the War of Ideas
John Blundell
Occasional Paper 119
ISBN 0 255 36500 4

The Changing Fortunes of Economic Liberalism
Yesterday, Today and Tomorrow
David Henderson
Occasional Paper 105 (new edition)
ISBN 0 255 36520 9

The Global Education Industry
Lessons from Private Education in Developing Countries
James Tooley
Hobart Paper 141 (new edition)
ISBN 0 255 36503 9

Saving Our Streams

The Role of the Anglers' Conservation Association in
Protecting English and Welsh Rivers
Roger Bate
Research Monograph 53
ISBN 0 255 36494 6

Better Off Out?

The Benefits or Costs of EU Membership
Brian Hindley & Martin Howe
Occasional Paper 99 (new edition)
ISBN 0 255 36502 0

Buckingham at 25

Freeing the Universities from State Control
Edited by James Tooley
Readings 55
ISBN 0 255 36512 8

Lectures on Regulatory and Competition Policy
Irwin M. Stelzer
Occasional Paper 120
ISBN 0 255 36511 X

Misguided Virtue
False Notions of Corporate Social Responsibility
David Henderson
Hobart Paper 142
ISBN 0 255 36510 1

To order copies of currently available IEA papers, or to enquire about availability, please contact:

Lavis Marketing
73 Lime Walk
Oxford OX3 7AD

Tel: 01865 767575
Fax: 01865 750079
Email: orders@lavismarketing.co.uk